Plains to the Pacific

The Life Story of Robert J. Slothower

Robert J. Slothower
and
James R. Harman

ISBN 978-1-64670-197-1 (Paperback)
ISBN 978-1-68526-854-1 (Hardcover)
ISBN 978-1-64670-198-8 (Digital)

Copyright © 2021 Robert J. Slothower and James R. Harman
All rights reserved
Second Edition

All rights reserved. No part of this publication may be reproduced, distributed, or transmitted in any form or by any means, including photocopying, recording, or other electronic or mechanical methods without the prior written permission of the publisher. For permission requests, solicit the publisher via the address below.

Covenant Books
11661 Hwy 707
Murrells Inlet, SC 29576
www.covenantbooks.com

Contents

Foreword 5
Introduction and Dedication 7
Kansas Prairie Years 9
Reunited in Denver 51
Ranching and Tragedy in Wyoming 92
Starting Over in Washington 159
Afterthoughts 191
Postscript and Robert's Poem 201
Historical Connections 207
Photo Section 224
Robert's Brothers 253
Trips to the Wyoming Homesteads 288
From Tea and Crumpets to Sage and Lightning ... 331
Robert's Family and the Civil War 344
Sources and Credits 357

Foreword

By Catherine Langrehr of IndieReader

IndieReader 2017 Discovery Award Winner. Spiritual and inspirational category for nonfiction: April 21, 2017 in Indie book reviews, inspirational/spiritual, approved, memoir, nonfiction by IR staff, five-star rating.

Plains to the Pacific by Robert J. Slothower and James R. Harman is a well-written and gripping time-capsule account of a lost world. Slothower has a literary style comparable to Hemingway's. There is a barely a wasted word in this invaluable document.

Verdict: Plains to the Pacific is an engaging read, the tale of a man who survived more hardship and excitement before he was thirty than most of us will ever experience in our lifetime.

Robert Slothower was born in 1871 on a farm in Nebraska, the third of five siblings. This book is the story of his long and adventurous life, from a childhood spent as near-slave labor to another family due to his own parents' poverty, through the minimal education he was able to gain in a one-room schoolhouse, to adult life in Denver, Wyoming, and Washington as a farmer, rancher, carpenter, musician, and whatever else he could turn his hand to. His autobiography has been edited and presented, with supplemental background material, by his great-grandson Jay Harman, the son of Slothower's eldest daughter's son.

Plains to the Pacific is an entertaining historical adventure, all the more appealing for being true. Slothower's style is laconic and relaxed, as if he were telling stories around the campfire, jumping from one tale to the next in a roughly chronological but unpolished, folksy style that adds to the book's grandfatherly charm. Whether it's the tale of how his younger brother Elmer lost some fingers to an axe or how his horse, Old Blue, decided to give a spontaneous bucking exhibition in the middle of a Fourth of July celebration, the tragic death of his first wife from acute appendicitis or the births of his children, Slothower relates each tale with the same dry, gentle, thoughtful tone, as a man who has seen it all and successfully recovered from most of it.

His most fervently emotional writing is reserved primarily for his family and for his conversion to a deep Christian faith. The moral principles that resonate through his writing—the value of hard work, kindness, service to others, gratitude for one's blessings, and willingness to press on through the more painful times—are sound and worthy of respect. His writing offers a valuable primary source for historians studying the post-Civil War period and America's westward expansion. Harman contributes additional depth to his great-grandfather's story with the appendices, containing some useful biographical and family details, filling in the life stories of Slothower's brothers, adding family pictures, and discussing the service of Slothower's father, three uncles, father-in-law, and grandfather in the Union Army during the Civil War.

Introduction and Dedication

by Robert J. Slothower

As the years passed, I have told my family of many experiences from my early life, and it seemed interesting enough to them that they thought it a good idea for me to write a sort of story of my life. So at last, I have decided to see what I can do about it, as the time has come in my life when I must lay down the shovel and the hoe and try to content myself with things that don't require much physical exertion. So hoping that my memory will serve me reasonably well, I will try to write my first, and no doubt my last story, based on facts taken from my life's experiences, good and bad, and at times rather humorous.

To my dear wife, Leonia, who has been such a wonderful wife and mother through the years, and to Pearl and Fred, my two oldest, and to Walter and Charles, my triplet boys, this story is lovingly dedicated.

Robert — January 2, 1946

Boy on Horse by Zach Franzen

Kansas Prairie Years

I was born near Omaha, Nebraska, on December 30, 1871. I was the third in a family of five, with a brother and a sister older, and a brother and a sister younger. My father and mother came west from Pennsylvania when my oldest brother, Aaron, was just a baby, and they lived at the Nebraska home until I was just about eighteen months old (so they said). I can't remember that far back, but I do have a very dim recollection of crossing a wide river on a ferryboat, which seems rather hard to believe of one so young. Nevertheless, this scene was stamped on my memory as the very first that I can remember. I can still see the old muddy water and the growth of some kinds of brush on the banks. Perhaps I was scared, as infants often are, and this may have been the cause of this unusual feat of recollection.

Well, it was the old Missouri River, and my folks were on their way with all their belongings (including three children) piled onto the old prairie schooner. They were moving out to the Kansas plains where my father had taken up a 160-acre homestead. I am not going into details of this trip into Kansas as I was most likely asleep most of the time, tucked away amongst the household goods, etc. (such as they were). There are two things that happened before we arrived at our destination that are stamped in my memory as definitely as the river scene, and again, perhaps it was the terrible fear that left these lasting impressions.

One evening, my father drove into what seemed to me a bend in a small creek and pulled off the road and made camp in a place where the long dry grass was pretty high. I suppose he thought he could burn off a place large enough to build the campfire, and so he did. Once he started it, he was unable to beat the fire out, and it got away and burned just about everything they had. I can't tell you the actual details of this calamity, but I know from hearing them tell about it in later years that it practically left them with nothing out there on the Kansas plains. There was no help very handy, as Kansas was very thinly settled at that time. I know that Father carried the scars of this experience, as Mother said I was almost lost in that fire.

We will never know or appreciate what sacrifices and suffering our fathers and mothers went through in the early days just to keep our bodies and souls together. We are too likely to look at the mistakes and bad things they have made and done and forget the many wonderful things they have done for us. Also, we must not forget the conditions under which they labored, about which I will tell you more as this real-life story progresses.

I do not know how the folks got over the rest of the journey, but I can remember them talking of some good people who were willing to help them to the best of their abilities. And by the way, I have never lived in a community in this "good old USA," no matter how godforsaken it seemed to be, that there were not some of God's chosen there to help in time of need, if only they knew where the help was needed.

Well, when my folks got to within a day or so drive of the homestead, they left me with some friends they had made somewhere along the way. They went on out ahead to build the house and make things ready. I suppose they left me behind because they thought I was too young to be of much help or that I might be lost down a badger hole or bitten by a rattler or carried off by a coyote, or something.

My recollection of this family that had me in their charge is very brief, although I will never forget when they hung me up by the heels to the ridgepole and just about scared the life out of me, but didn't hurt me very much. Which goes to prove, along with my other two recounted experiences, that it sometimes takes a good scare to make a child remember some things, but please, don't try it out on my grandchildren. I do not know why they hung me wrong end up, but I guess they were just trying to get me adjusted to the heat, cold, and position. This was all very necessary for the early settlers in Kansas, especially regarding the heat.

I don't know how long I was with this family, but what I am going to tell you from now on, I hope I remember more clearly. The first home that I ever had on this earth was of the earth, "earthly" as Paul said of the first Adam. It was just a square hole cut out of the side of a bank, with a doorway dug out on a level with the bottom of the house. The floor and walls were just dirt. The roof was put on by first placing ridge logs at different places and then poles placed on top of the logs, laid as close together as was possible to lay them. Then came a layer of straw or hay and then more dirt. The only window was a very small one in the back of the house. This window was placed high up in the center, which let in just enough light to enable us to see our way about.

Our light for the night was made by braiding some string together, which was torn from some old garments that had served their purpose and, henceforth, were good for nothing else but to make wicks for the light source. This was called a "witch." A shallow vessel was partly filled with grease, and the wick was laid in that and propped up over the side of the vessel and lit the same as the old kerosene lamps. And how the wicks sputtered and waved in the breeze! Of course, this was just a makeshift until we got the kerosene lamp, which served its purpose for so many years.

I remember the walls of our residence were full of holes of different sizes made by different burrowing animals that had inhabited the soil before we dug in. Sometimes, they would show up in the holes, as if to contest our right to who had the priority. It was not so bad, unless it happened to be a skunk or a rattler, of which the latter were very much in evidence in Kansas in those days.

My father was a carpenter, and whenever people got enough cottonwood boards together to build some kind of shack, he would often lend a hand with the building. This made it necessary for him to be absent from us once in a while.

At one time, there was a band of Omaha Indians (supposedly civilized) who were camped in a grove about three quarters of a mile from our place. They were surely pests, especially when they happened to get possession of whiskey, which they did not know how to handle very well. It soon got the upper hand of them and caused them to forget that they were supposed to be civilized. One day, five of them came to our house when Father was away. They were pretty drunk and armed with six-shooters. Well, I guess just to keep them in good humor, Mother fixed them some dinner, and while they were eating, the whiskey got the upper hand, and they commenced to shoot up through the roof. The dirt came down in streams and all over the table, as well as everything in the room.

Meanwhile, I was cached away behind some goods boxes in the corner, just about scared to death and thinking I might be the next target. Then Mother spoke something to them in the Indian tongue, of which she had a very limited knowledge, and they put up their guns and left. I have often thought of that scene and wondered what she said to them, wishing that I possessed those magic words to use on some outlaws I have seen in my time. My mother was a small woman, but she must have had great power of speech on certain occasions. Had Father been at home, there would have been a fight, no doubt.

I do not remember how long we lived in the old dugout, but I must have been three or four years old when Father started to build a stone house. Sometimes he would let me go with him to the quarry, where he took the stone out in big blocks, loaded them onto the wagon, and hauled them away, a few blocks at a load.

We had to cross the Solomon River, which had a soft sandy bottom. Often, the wagon would bog down and stall the team, which would force him to unload some of the rock before they could pull it out. And I suppose those heavy stones are still there, buried in the sand, as sleeping memorials of the hard struggles of the Kansas pioneer. These covered artifacts, like so many of our efforts, remain hidden away where no one can see or appreciate them, while the stones built into structures out in the sight of men will be remembered, when even those who built them are forgotten.

After collecting the stones came the building of the walls. It must have been a long tiresome job, shaping up and placing those heavy stones, but Father was a very good stonemason, as well as general handyman, which was so necessary for the pioneer. In time, the four walls were up and the roof was on, and it was just one big room with a board partition across somewhere near the center. The ceiling joists were placed overhead and some loose boards were placed on top of the joists, just to keep them out of the weather for future use. Cottonwood lumber has a way of twisting and warping all out of shape in a very short time if exposed to the weather. Laying the floor and putting in the door and windows was about as far as Father ever got with that house, which was our dwelling place until I was nine years old. During that time, some very interesting things took place, which I will tell you about in turn as I can recall them.

First, Father dug a well and struck solid rock in just about the depth that he should have found water, and he was pretty badly discouraged. He kept pounding away for several days, and every one of us was anxiously awaiting for results when a loud yell came up (through the sixty-five-foot hole) to pull him out quickly! Somehow, we were able to pull him up out of the well in time. When Dad, very much excited, told us what had happened, we were all very happy. He said he was pounding away with the pick in the rock bottom, when the point of the pick finally broke through, and the water came in so fast that he was afraid he would be drowned before they could get him out. I lived in that community until I was seventeen years old, and I never heard of that well failing in its supply of good cold clear water.

Father did some farming with very fair results when there was sufficient rainfall. I will say that barring drought, hailstorms, grasshoppers, and potato bugs, the Kansas prairie soil produced some fine crops. I recall with a great deal of pleasure the harvest times. I remember the old grain cradle and the hand-bound bundles, the neighbors trading work to help each other, and the women fixing up a big feed of such things as the farm could produce. We never saw much money change hands, but people seemed pretty happy most of the time.

I remember how the ladies used to fix up a big bucket of lemonade ice-cold and take it out to the men working in the field. They brought it out around the middle of the forenoon and again in the afternoon, and in a very short period, the lemonade was all gone. I was one of the grateful crew. You, no doubt, wonder how the lemonade was made to be so cold. Well, they cut the ice on the river and stored it away for summer use. You can believe that ice was very much appreciated during the hot summer months. I don't know how they got the lemons at that time, but later on, when the railroad came, it was much easier to get things from the outside.

Father somehow bought the first "team-drawn" harvester that I ever saw. It was a rear-cut mowing machine with a reaper attachment, consisting of a reel and a dropping device, which was attached to the back of the cutter bar in such a way that it dropped the grain in bundles the full width of the swath. It made it necessary to bind the grain up in stations by hand, and this was done by placing men around the field in different places. When the machine came around again, the way would be clear for the next swath. Just another step in the evolution of the great combines we see in the fields today in 1946.

The evolution of the combine also brings to mind the small beginnings of farm production in the state that would one day become the leading wheat-producing state in the Union. Dad and the machine were kept pretty busy for a while. When the grain was all cut he would just drop off the harvester attachment, and then he was ready for the hay, which grew wild at that time on the Kansas plains. It seemed to thrive pretty well even when the other crops failed on account of a drought or other causes, like grasshoppers for instance.

I remember one afternoon in the latter part of July or first part of August, when we had had a pretty hot dry spell. The sun seemed rather dim and looked like a big red ball of fire. At the same time, we commenced to hear a roaring sound like a windstorm approaching. There had not been a cloud in the sky, and we were all puzzled as to what it was all about. All at once we found out, for grasshoppers commenced to land on everything in sight until everything was completely covered. They didn't stop eating until they had consumed nearly everything they could eat. There was nothing left of the corn stalks but stubs; the grass was all gone, and the country was a picture of desolation. I don't know how long it took them to clean up everything that had been growing, but I can remember very well the event that was the end of them.

One hot day when the sun seemed bent on burning up anything that might be left, we noticed big white-capped clouds commencing to roll up from all sides. To anyone who has never seen a storm gather out on the plains, I will say that they have missed one of the most inspiring sights that a person ever beheld. These clouds seemed to tower miles high, and the tops were so bright they dazzled the eyes.

They seemed to march in from all sides until there was only a small patch of blue sky left overhead. Then lightning commenced to come down in great streaks, and thunder shook the earth. The clouds turned black and then green, and then hail, as large as a small cup began to fall. Just a few at first and then smaller and more of them, until the ground was covered. Then it turned to rain, and the water commenced to run off into ravines and creeks.

The river rose and covered all the bottomland, and then it cleared off. Then sun came out and a rainbow appeared, and all was quiet again. But there were no grasshoppers and no corn either, and another year of hard times was before us. I remember walking along the river over drifts of almost solid grasshoppers, and these drifts stuck around for a long time. This is a description of just one Kansas hailstorm I had to experience. There were so many of them, and sometimes I had no choice but to stand outside in the storm and take all that was coming down, being beaten with the hail and getting soaked to the skin.

The railroad finally came through and cut our farm in two, which wasn't as bad as it might have been. It left our house and other buildings, such as they were, and most of the farm itself, on the handy side of the road. It was only a branch line with about one combination train a day. I remember the day my older brother and I walked all the way to town, which was about four miles. This was to see the first train and railroad engine I ever did see. They were soon making their daily trips right through our farm!

There was a steep grade where they used to get stuck when the grasshoppers got on the track and greased the rails. It was a great source of amusement for us to see the little red locomotive's drive wheels spin around while it hissed and puffed, and then watch it back up and try again, maybe trying several times before making the grade. Then we would crawl under the bridge and let the train run over us. When I think of those things, I wonder at how little a thing it took to amuse people, especially children in those days, and how hard it is to amuse them now. There are so many things to interest people now, and still they are never satisfied. What would we do today if we were cut off from the modern conveniences and made to live like our forefathers?

It was about this time that the Sioux Indians went on the warpath and killed several families, some within ten miles of us. The settlers were pretty badly scared up over it. One day, I remember the soldiers came marching by on the road just north of our place. We could see them very plainly marching two abreast, going out west to fight the Indians. After that, there were no more Indian scares around there.

My story would not be complete if I did not say something about the prairie fires that swept across the country before there were many plowed fields to check them. Many settlers lost their homes and all they had to keep house with, and sometimes they lost their lives. When a fire got started in a high wind, it was a terrible thing to see and experience, especially at night. The whole sky would light up and red flames and yellow and black smoke would roll across the land. It never lasted long, like a timber fire, and was over and gone rather quickly, but what a black scene of desolation it left behind.

I have gone over the land after one of these fires and seen many dead snakes and small animals that had been caught and burned to death before they could reach a place of refuge, usually some kind of hole in the ground. Farmers generally would safeguard themselves against prairie fires by making what they called fireguards. It was done by plowing a few furrows around the buildings, and then again farther out, and sometimes when there was no wind, they would burn out the dry grass between the furrows.

Things went along pretty well on the old prairie farm for a while, and then things began to happen. The crops began to fail more frequently, and sickness came along. I remember when they put me to bed with a high fever and the old homeopathic doctor was called in. The doctor said, "It's typhoid fever!" I can't pass this old doctor up without a word for him because I'm sure both I and my younger brother owe our lives to him. He was a strange old character with a long white beard. I should judge he was past seventy years old. He rode a pinto or spotted pony, and with his medicine bags strapped across his saddle and his whiskers waving in the breeze, he would hit it out across the countryside any old time of day or night as fast as his old pinto could carry him. He would attend the sick and do what he could to help along his noble profession and never said much about money that I know of. There were many who owed their lives to old Doc Landen, especially among the children.

The last thing I remember was that the sun was rising in the west and the moon was setting in the east, and that everything was all "topsy-turvy." Then everything went black and I never did learn how long I was unconscious. When I came to, Mother was bending over me and said, "Thank God, he will live!" Well, I was pretty sick and weak, and it was some time before I could even walk again. They said I ended up actually having pneumonia.

One day when I could walk around a little, I wanted to go down to the creek and catch a fish, so my older brother took me in charge and steered me down there and back. I didn't catch a fish that time, but I should tell you that fishing was my favorite sport or pastime when I was a boy. I would sit on the bank all day just to see the cork bob up and down, and sometimes I would bring them in. One time several years later, I caught a six-pound channel catfish which is the largest fish I have ever caught to date. Maybe someday I will catch a bigger one yet!

There was a grist mill on the river, about three miles or so from our place. It was run by waterpower. I remember one time we didn't have much to eat in the house and we rushed the season somewhat. We went out in the cornfield and picked some corn that was not yet ripe, then we stayed up late that night, shucking a sack. It was so green that we had to twist some of it off the cob. Then Aaron and I took the old team and drove to the mill the next morning and got it ground. The miller got his pay by taking out a toll of meal, which was very small pay.

I watched that corn go through the fanning mill and down a long wooden spout, then into the big revolving stones, and come out cornmeal on the other side. I got a great kick out of watching it. I still had to eat my portion of it, and I didn't like it too well at the time, for cornmeal was very common stuff for us kids. There were many times when that was about all we had to eat.

I suppose I should say something of the social life of those times. I don't think that it differed very much from the social life of any frontier community of those early days. It revolved around the common "old time" dances, with people coming from many miles away to gather in different homes and dance all night to the music of an "old time" fiddler. By the way, the famous Buffalo Girls, for which the old dance tune was composed, once danced in our old home, but I have forgotten their real names.

It was a happy time for me when I could find a place somewhere out of the way and sit and listen to the fiddler, and sometimes the banjo. Little did I dream then that I would be playing the same old tunes with my brother on another frontier under somewhat different circumstances. This would turn out to be in the heart of the Wyoming Rocky Mountains many years later.

Later on, they organized what they called a literary society which met once a week in the schoolhouse. It was a one-room building which was built after the period about which I have been writing. They would have a debate on some subject, and leaders would be appointed. The leaders would each choose two speakers, and they would argue the question from every angle that they could think of. Three judges would decide the winner. Sometimes the discussion would become so bitter that they would almost come to blows, but generally, they would cool off and get ready for the next week's session. Then there was a fifteen-minute recess, and they would take time out to prepare a program for the upcoming week and do some visiting. Next, they would have a program consisting of songs, recitations, and dialogues. After that, they would be dismissed and go home, often singing some old familiar songs, accompanied by the rattle and squeak of the old lumber wagon in which they were riding. Those wagon rides were something to be remembered. They would throw a few forks of hay in the wagon box, and as many as could crowd in just sat around on the hay. I suppose there were many matches struck during these rather close associations of mortal beings.

I have gotten ahead of my story and must go back to the realities of things that were happening at that time. Some things that would be better forgotten, perhaps if it were possible, but the bitter must be taken with the sweet, so here goes.

Times got very hard on the homestead, owing to crop failures and other misfortunes. I was too young to understand what it was all about. I do know that the largest percentage of the early settlers in Kansas had to give up and leave because they were unable to make a living for their families. Anyway, my father and we three boys stayed on the old place and tried to live there and "batch it" for a while. (Robert's mother had taken his little sister Cora with her to Denver.) It was a tough job, as Father was away working most of the time, and we three boys were left to our own resources, which were not much. I cannot remember how long things were like this, but it seemed an age to me.

My older brother Aaron was very mechanically minded and was always fixing up some sort of machine to make a big noise. He conceived the idea of making wooden windmills and putting them up on posts, with a tin can attached in such a way that it would make such a rattling and banging noise that they could be heard all over the place. Not satisfied with making the noise outside, he went to work on the inside. He stuck up spools of different sizes on nails all over the board partition, and then made a large wheel with a groove in the center as a drive wheel, which had a crank on it. A twist of the crank would set the whole business in operation, and it made a noise like a train going over a trestle. Well, we got a great kick out of it for a while, but like all other amusements, it grew old, so then he turned his attention to making wagons. Some of these wagons would have done credit to a grown man. It was almost a perfect duplicate of a real wagon of those times.

Aaron is now seventy-eight years old and is still making things that are useful for the farmers of our community. He seems to like it as well as he did then. He has his own shop in which all the machines have been made by his own hands, with the exception of an old Ford engine that provides the power to run all the rest.

Aaron was also our cook, being the oldest, and he was about as good (or bad) at experimenting on us kids with his cooking as he was with the machines. After my long spell of sickness, too much vinegar gravy did not agree with me, but I had to take it until the fad wore out. Then about the time when cornbread made without shortening or leavening powder was getting pretty old, my older sister Edith, who had been staying with a family down east awhile, came home. Although she was only a girl of ten years or so, she seemed to have accumulated a lot of knowledge badly needed around our home at that time. When she took on the responsibility of running the kitchen and made a batch of real white flour biscuits, I thought she was the best-looking person I had ever seen, and life started to feel a bit more worthwhile.

We had to clean up a little, which was not so hard to take, as it was only about one-fourth mile to the old swimming hole, and there was plenty of sand on the bottom which done very well when soap was scarce. Things went along pretty well for a while, but then winter came along. We kids had to go cut and rustle wood to keep from freezing and to cook what little grub we had.

There was a grove of cottonwood trees about a quarter mile from our house on what we called "Skunk Creek." This creek, most of the way, was a wet weather creek, not having much water in it except through the rainy season. There was a rather deep hole in the creek bottom in the midst of those trees. We often used this spot for a swimming hole during the hot summers. It never quite dried up entirely.

We thought we would take the axe and go down there and see if we could rustle a few dry limbs for firewood. As it was, all four of us volunteered to go. We found that the pond had frozen over and the water had seeped away to a certain extent, leaving the ice in a kind of dish shape sloping toward the center. We had all gone out onto the ice first thing, as kids generally do, and then Elmer, who was only about five years old, somehow got possession of the axe. We tried to get it away from him, but he started to run with it.

Just as he got to the edge of the ice, his feet slipped out from under him, and he fell forward, throwing out his hands to catch himself. The axe came down and cut off the first, second, and a piece of the third finger of his right hand. Well, you can imagine what an excited bunch we kids were, with Father away at work and four miles to a doctor. So I guess we did all we knew how to do, and that might have been the wrong thing. We took him to the house, put his hand in a pan of cold water and just left it there while Aaron went after Dad. When Dad got home, he had a neighbor go for the doctor. He didn't get there until late at night and dressed and fixed up the hand. We were all pretty badly put out and feeling a little like we were to blame for letting him get the axe, but that is just another one of those things that couldn't be helped after it was done.

Elmer afterward became an old-time fiddler, and I have heard him say that he was glad that it wasn't his left hand that got crippled, which would have made it hard for him to become a fiddler. I have heard him pick the banjo some with what stubs he has left, which goes to show that where there is a will, there is a way. He still loves to play the violin, and furthermore, he makes his own violins. I will say more about this later on in my story, trying to go back now to where we were just kids, back on the Kansas plains.

As to what happened during the next year or so, I do not remember very clearly. We lived on somehow in the old place without a mother, and, it seemed, without a father most of the time. Finally, Dad gave up trying to keep us boys and Edith together any longer. We were placed in different homes. Father and my oldest brother joined a party that was going out to Colorado to cut railroad ties out there in the mountains. That was a very sad and lonely part of my life, but not so bad as what was yet to follow. Elmer and I were still together, with an old crippled lady who was very hard up, just like the rest of us. Her husband had gone west with the many other men who had gone, in hopes of earning enough money to keep their families from starving. Somehow, the money was a long time getting there and we had very little to eat, while our clothes, such as they were, were getting pretty well-worn.

I will never forget how a typical Christmas went for us children. And we never did forget to hang up our stockings, as had always been our custom. Father and Mother had always done everything they could to make Christmas a happy time for us. I can remember the candy toys, such as brightly colored chickens, dogs, and cats. And the different candy ornaments, which we thought were too pretty to eat. We would set them aside so we could look at them and perhaps worship them until the mixed and stick candies were all gone. Then the temptation would get so strong that we would commence to nibble on the idols and so spoiled their beauty that there was nothing left to do but finish them off. The red-top, copper-toed boots, the little highly-colored garments, Dad acting as Old St. Nick, all those things were attended to, and I'm sure at somewhat of a sacrifice on their part. It will always remain fresh in my memory as the happiest time of my childhood days.

On this Christmas sixty-four years ago, when we looked in our stockings there was just one penny stick of peppermint candy. Of course, you can imagine how disappointed we were and it took a long time to get over our feelings, but we didn't blame anyone even then. Since then, I have good cause to remember that poor old lady was not financially able to be a very liberal Santa Claus. I guess we were a great source of annoyance to this woman, for she had long since raised her family. It was only natural that she resented taking on a second bunch.

She was inclined to be a little cranky at times, especially when one day we two boys were foraging around to see what we could find to drive away the monotony. That's when we ran across one of those cats that has a stripe down his back and a bushy tail. We thought that we might get some kind of a verbal reward if we could exterminate him or her, such as the case may be. While Elmer watched the cat, I went to find a suitable weapon and finally came back with a pole that I thought had a longer range than the animal, but I was underestimating its range by quite a bit. By the time we succeeded in dispatching this animal, we were just about as badly scented up as the cat. When we went to the house to get our reward, the old lady gave it to us by keeping us out of the house until suitable improvements could be made.

About this time, the old lady said she could not afford to keep us any longer. Elmer went to live with her daughter whose husband was also one of the railroad tie party, and who had a family of littler girls. This good-hearted lady had room for just one until different arrangements could be made. I was taken in by a family by the name of "S" (we will call them), which was to be my home for seven years, which seemed to me then, to be a very long period of time.

S's farm joined our old farm. I could look across and see the old stone house and the old cottonwood grove, and it was a constant reminder of my childhood days. Should I have been planted away in some strange part of the country, I should have been more likely to forget some of the things that would have been better forgotten.

The following spring, Father came back from Colorado and found a suitable place for my sister Edith, about seven miles away in one direction, and a place for Elmer fourteen miles in another. We were separated, and in all those years we very seldom saw each other. The loneliness that came over me and haunted me day and night for many months, I can never forget. The days seemed as though they would never end, and I was always looking for the time to come when our family would be together again. From my own experience, I can imagine the feelings of my own children who have grown up and scattered with families of their own, and just why they are so anxious to get home once in a while to the place which had been a home for all of them for so many years. The difference is, we were forced out, while they went out on their own after we had done what we could for them to try to fit them for a place in the world.

Up to this time, I had not had the chance to go to school very much, but from now on I was to go to school for three months every winter. During this time there was not as much to do on the farm, but the rest of the children went the full term. So if my spelling is bad and my vocabulary is not so good, please remember that while other children were in school, I was working on the farm. I was either out herding cattle, out following the plow, working in the harvest field, or doing the 101 things that urgently had to be done on the farm.

I was not a privileged character or a hired servant, but rather a slave. I got my meals (better than I had been having) and the clothes that hung on my back, but I did not have any shoes six months of the year. I received a good scolding and sometimes a licking if I failed to do what was expected of me. This was my pay for over seven years. When I finally made up my mind to leave, the only way I could get the money to pay my fare was to sell my saddle pony for about half price.

When I look back over the heartbreaking loneliness and hard knocks of those seven years, it is painfully clear that the only interest my master had in me was to get out of me all the work and profit that he could, taking full advantage of my unfortunate position for his own personal benefit. Still, I would be ungrateful not to mention the fact that he did give me my first lesson in writing that I remember. He was a very good writer, and I wish I could do as well as he could instead of this pitiful scrawl. He would make the copy for me, and then I would try to make the letters as near like his as was possible. I suppose even today, my handwriting bears a slight resemblance to the original copy, regardless of the spelling.

One of the first things I remember doing in the way of work was working on the woodpile. He persuaded me that if I got up early and worked at cutting wood, I would work up a good appetite for breakfast. In so doing, I would become a strong man—the ambition of every boy, I am sure. As I had not altogether recovered from my bad sick spell, this idea appealed to me. So one morning after doing my usual chores, I started work with an old dull axe, and the wood was hard dry ash poles. After I had hacked all around a stick, it looked just about like a beaver had been working on it but with no results. Then I got mad and leaned it up against the block and hit it as hard as I could with the back of the axe. It flew up, and the slivered end struck me in the right eye, almost knocking me out. The blood ran down my face and I got so sick I nearly fainted. My eye was blind for a long time after that, and I thought I would never be able to see with it again. But one day, when I was out herding cattle, I began to see things very dimly at first, then gradually plainer, until the eye was all right again.

It seemed I didn't need both eyes to be qualified to herd cattle, so this was my main job as a starter on my road to usefulness, that was until I got big enough to drive a team. Then they built a wire fence, which ended my lonely days on the herd ground. I don't know just how long I herded, but I must tell you something of my experiences out there all by myself. Wet to the skin in the cold rainy days of the early spring, when it rained and snowed sometimes for four or five days at a time, I would stand and shiver with the cold, watch the mud ooze out between my toes (I was barefooted), and wonder if the day would ever end. Then would come the long, dry, hot summer, with the sun beating down hard as it can out on the Kansas plains. Such experiences taught me to search the sky for the least speck of a cloud, in hopes it might offer some small relief from the terrible heat. In doing so, I learned to study the clouds, and that became one of the most inspiring studies of my life. I can say that in all the different places I have been, there is no place that can compare with Kansas for the beauty and inspiring terribleness of the clouds.

I watched for hours the approach of a storm, and by taking note of the shape of the cloud and the direction it was going, I learned to tell with a pretty good degree of accuracy whether it would cast its shadows my way or not. Sometimes, it would leave me standing in the sun and go on its way to bless some other part of the great expanse of prairie. I would wonder whether it would develop into one of those twisters that were so greatly feared, or perhaps a hailstorm, such as I have already described. Maybe it would be a hard soaking rain that would sweep across the country like the waves of the sea. Maybe just another dry blowout, or an electrical storm with little or no rain, when one was expecting another Noah's flood. It would finally break away, with not even enough rain to lay the dust after thunder and flashes of bright lightning that sometimes went on for hours.

How much different it was then compared to our present location in the state of Washington where it will rain for days at a time and we will say nothing about it, just like how some people make a great noise and do nothing, while others carry on the work of the world and say nothing much about it.

While the clouds here come up quickly, spend their contents, and are gone, on the plains their progress is slow. It will sometimes take many hours for a cloud to develop into a rain or hailstorm and complete its progress across the sky. I remember one morning, I looked out across the northwest horizon and saw a very bright bank of clouds rising out there and told the folks that it would hail before night. Of course, they laughed at the foolish little boy making such a prophecy, but my cloudbank kept rising bigger and higher, until later in the afternoon, it turned loose and fulfilled my prophecy. I rather thought they would ask me how I knew so much about it, but nothing was said, so I didn't get the credit for that storm.

I was told that the great Methodist Bishop Quayle wrote a book about Kansas clouds, which I someday wish to read. You may think I am a little batty about clouds, but they were my greatest friends for over seven years, and in the summer when they did not appear, I was very lonely. Sometimes they would turn loose and give me a good beating, but that was much better than being left alone. Perhaps God would forgive me if I should quote the familiar Psalm 121:1–2. The word *clouds* instead of *hills* reminds us that our help comes from the God who made them both.

Well, around this time, I got another friend. They got me a small shepherd pup, so small that I had to carry him around in my arms at first until he was old enough to navigate for himself. Our friendship became mutual as he grew up. I taught him how to drive the cattle and round them up, and if one of them got out of the bunch, he would bring them back. And if a strange animal came around, he would run it off. He was a big help to me, but he wouldn't work for the boss or anyone else. He (the boss, I mean) didn't like that very much.

When my dog (Rover, I called him) got to be grown up, he got the habit of running after rabbits. One day as I was herding the cattle near the railroad tracks, I lost sight of him as the train approached and later went to look for him. I found half of him on one side of the rails, and the other half on the other side, still kicking. And so departed my constant friend and helper. Only a boy that has lost his dog can know or appreciate how I felt. It was a tragic affair for a small boy to experience.

I was getting quite a good-sized herd of cattle by this time, and it was a pretty hard job to herd them on foot without Rover, so they got me a little bay pony. She and I carried on the herding job until the pasture was built, which was 160 acres fenced in by three strands of barbed wire. This was the first of this kind of fencing I had ever seen, and it ruined many a good horse until they got used to it. Not only were the horses badly cut up by running into it, but lots of stock were killed by lightning when it would strike the wire and follow it around, killing anything that was close to the fence.

I must also tell you something of the old district school, just a one-room frame building, but large enough to accommodate the pupils of the district. It served all ages from about six years to about seventeen or eighteen, with one teacher to take care of the whole school. There were about forty pupils in all, if memory serves me right. The teacher received about forty dollars per month for what surely had to be a tough job, trying to teach all classes and trying to keep some sort of order. And teaching a variety of pupils ranging from little ones to the school bullies of which there were three. These three bullies had arranged themselves together in such a way that they just about ran the whole school and the teacher too.

The teacher was usually some young girl teaching her first or second term. Well, they took a dislike to me and just about had me scared out of there, and if I had had my way, I would have left school and never come back. But it was the rule that everyone should have some sort of education, so I was forced to take a lot of abuse from those three boys, who also caused the teacher a lot of trouble. She took my part and was a good friend to me, and by the way, it is a good thing when there is a person, once in a while, who is willing to take the part of the "underdog" in order that he, "the underdog," may get the support needed to properly grow up.

Those boys had the habit of following me out at recess or at the noon hour, and then running me off of the school grounds to the point that my inferiority complex was just about getting me down. One day, I got to thinking that I would have to take a stand, even if I failed, so this was the way it happened. The biggest of those three boys wore an old-fashioned long scarf looped around his neck, with the ends hanging down his back. Now the schoolhouse door was right in the corner of the building and about two steps above the ground. So at recess time, I hurried out with the big boy following, as usual, although this time, instead of running away, I stepped to one side and grabbed those two scarf ends giving him a hard swing. This landed him flat on his back, and then I climbed on top of him, trying my best to beat him up good, but he was so strong that I did not succeed in doing him much damage. But I held him down until the bell rang, and when he managed to get up and we exchanged a few blows, and he got a little of the best of it. That settled the bluffing and we remained good friends from then on until I left the country. I think we even exchanged a few letters after I came west, and I will always have a sort of respect for the other boys for not interfering with our little scrap. I think that young teacher wore a very pleased smile when she looked at me afterward. She was only a girl and a mighty sweet one, and I was just about old enough to commence to appreciate a pleasant smile from a pretty young girl, especially when the smiles for me were so few and far between.

I will never forget this teacher and her kindness to me, as she seemed to understand that school privileges had been very limited for me. And when I was working on a particularly hard problem and she kept me after school, it was no punishment to me when she would sit down beside me and lay one arm across my shoulders while trying to help me with the problem. Even beyond my educational experience, I owe more to her than to almost any other living being. She was one of about three people who showed a genuine, sympathetic understanding of my life at that time and acted accordingly. I wish there were more people in the world today willing to spend a little more time with the underprivileged. She was also my last teacher, as I recall, or maybe I had one man teacher after her, but he didn't count.

Well, I guess at this point, I had better go back to the farm again, as that is where I got my start in real hard knocks, educationally at least. First, I will say something about the premises I inhabited during my years of servitude. It was a two-room house, the main room being built of lumber, the boards standing on end, with some kind of mortar between them. Then there was a side room used as a kitchen and eating room, which was built of sod and covered with dirt and a kind of pale rock. This rock was rather useless as a barrier to rainwater if it rained for several days. It would forget to quit leaking water when it stopped raining outside. That was the extent of our dwelling for the over seven years that I lived there.

During the years I lived in that house, there were seven of us who ate and slept there, with all of us sleeping in the large room. Please don't think I am sounding ungrateful in telling of our housing conditions because this house was better than a lot of them were in those days. I am just trying to portray to modern readers what many of the older generation had to put up with.

If we are not quite satisfied with our place of abode, given all the modern conveniences most people have these days, it is merely the same spirit that made the pioneer settlers dissatisfied with things as they were then. This in turn prompted them to work and strive and plan for better things for the future. And so it is, the "spirit of progress," as it should be. We should take into consideration our great God and father of the universe, who works in all things that are good for us if we would only stop long enough to give him credit and praise for it all. Well, the trouble with most of us is we just take things for granted and leave God out of our lives. I'll share more of the spiritual side of life later, if God lets me live long enough.

There was a building lot comprised of nearly an acre, fenced in by an Osage orange hedge on three sides, which served as a windbreaker (sometimes). I must say that you have never seen a real fence until you have seen this kind of a hedge. If I were enclosing my place with an Osage orange hedge, I would want to be sure that the devil was on the outside before it grew up because he would never be able to get out unless he dug under or flew over. It was so full of thorns that a bird could not go through it. Inside this enclosure was the barn, corncribs, cattle shed, corral, pigpen, haystacks, and chicken house.

Then, close to the house, was a cyclone and vegetable cellar, a garden plot, an apple orchard that very seldom had any apples on it, and last but not least, a well, with the proverbial old oaken buckets and the squeaky old pulley at the top. This well was about fifty-five feet deep, and you can imagine what kind of a job it was to draw water by hand to water six head of workhorses, seventy-five to a hundred head of hogs, and a bunch of calves, as well as provide for family use. And I did the greatest share of it for all those years. The old squeaky pulley at the top ceased to be a song of praise. I could dwell on these things forever, but it would cease to be interesting. I must try to confine myself to the high spots for I have a long way to go before I get caught up to the present time, as I'm now seventy-four years old. Perhaps you will get tired of this story and cast it aside.

Well, after the cattle were fenced in, I was left free to work on the farm. I liked this much better, as it gave me more of a variety of jobs to do. My boss had a fine lot of good horses, and it was my job to learn to handle them and to help take care of them. This was very interesting to me, as I always liked good horses. I think about the first thing I learned to do with the team was plow, and what fun it was to follow the plow up and down the long furrows with the cool fresh earth caressing my bare feet, and then the harrow smoothing down the ground, getting it in shape for the marker for corn or wheat or some other small-grain crop and then follow it with the planter.

I will always remember the corn planter, for the day I took the measure, I sat on the corn planter all day watching the marks go by and giving the handle a little yank, this way and that, so that the corn would come up in rows both ways. My head was almost bursting and I was ready to keel over, when finally the field was finished. The next day, I was in bed where I remained for about a week or more, not much help to anyone.

Next would come the cultivating, which was nice work. They had a riding cultivator, but I always preferred the walking one because I liked to keep my feet on the ground. I could watch the ground curl up around the shovels and settle around the young plants, covering up what weeds the shovels would not take out. I always loved to work in the cornfield, and above all to husk the corn when it was ripe and to hear the ears bang against the bump board.

It was not all pleasant as you surely know, but perhaps it would be best not to tarry too long on the disagreeable things, as there is enough suffering in the world as it is. I will just mention one of the summers that comes to mind. The corn had grown to be nearly as high as my head and appeared a wonderful prospect for a good crop when there came up a hot wind from the south. Before the day was over the corn leaves were rattling like paper, and the crop was burned up and finished. That year as near as I can recall, Mr. "S" had to go into Nebraska to buy corn to feed the stock. That is just a picture from the other side again.

I have told you something of the early harvest scene, so will now tell you a bit about the early threshing scene. Steam or power-threshing machines were not known in that part of Kansas at that time as their machines were still being driven by horsepower. The separator itself was not so much different than the modern one, except that it was a much more cumbersome affair. Instead of the blower stacker of our times, it elevated the straw by a long carrier that had endless belts with slots across them, which carried the straw away from the machine.

Someone had to stack the straw by hand, and as a boy that was usually my job, and a dirty job it was. They would set the machine in such a way that the wind would blow the dust off the machine and the straw stacker got it all, or as much as he could hold and that was plenty. And the horsepower was a sort of a gear powered unit that was set at a distance from the separator. It was run by a tumbling shaft, which was connected to the horsepower and the cylinder of the machine by a large level gear. This part of the machine made a humming noise and could be heard for miles at times, so we could always tell when the threshing machine was working in the community.

The horsepower had a series of sweeps that extended out from the center, and a team of horses was hitched to each one. Usually, about fourteen to sixteen horses were used, and they simply went around in a circle with a driver in the center holding a long whip, which was used to touch up the lagging nags. A three-man crew went with the rig, while the rest of the crew were men on hand with their own teams there just to exchange work. In other words, you help me today, and I will help you tomorrow. And if one had a bigger job than another, I never heard of them quarreling about it.

When I got to be about sixteen years old, the separator boss thought it was time that I was promoted from the straw stack, so he called me up one morning to cut bands. I was feeling just fine about it when suddenly the band knife slipped, and I cut my thumb about half off. As with many of the mistakes we make in life, I can see the scar yet. I never cut bands again but went onto the stacks to pitch bundles.

There was no mechanical band cutter on those machines, and the bands were made of straw, twisted around and tied by more bands. The first grain binder I ever saw was an eight-foot Deering owned and ran by an old Negro who used five horses, with a little Black boy riding the lead horse. I thought it was the greatest machine I had ever seen outside of the separator.

It took my sore thumb a long time to heal up, as the knife was one of those kind with a blade edge like a ripsaw, which bore deeply into the flesh and bone. It was still pretty sore when I went to husking corn that fall and I got infection in it and was pretty badly discouraged, but it finally healed up without me losing much time. As long as I could earn my board and clothes and make some profit for the boss, that was all that was necessary.

People were very superstitious in those days. They used to sit around in the evening and tell ghost stories, and they had me so badly scared that I was afraid to go out at night. I must say that of all the fears that ever got a hold of a person, the fear of seeing a ghost has got to be the worst. I have feared for my life on several occasions, but I have never felt a more awful fear at any time in my life than I did in the experience that I am going to tell you about now.

The elderly father of "S" lived on the farm adjoining. After many years as a widower, he had married an old maid who was very homely. Not long after they were married, she was taken with TB (tuberculosis) of the quick variety. She had been very kind to me, but they would not allow me to see her until the morning after her death, when they told me I could now go over to the house if I wanted to, and of course I was anxious to see my old friend for the last time.

Well, she had died in a spasm of pain or horror and there were no undertakers to fix the deceased up in those days. I had never seen a dead person before and was not prepared for what I saw, almost fainting at the awful, changed expression of that face. It haunted me day and night for a long time, and even in my dreams, I could see that hideous face. But the worst of it came when the old man, who was sleeping there alone after her death, came over to our place one night in a terrible state of mind. He said that she had come back and was haunting him, so the next night, they made me go over and spend the night with him. I have never again spent such a night in my life looking constantly for ghosts, and in my imagination, seeing plenty of them while never sleeping a wink all night. I ended up staying with him every night for a week or so but never saw any more ghosts or heard of any coming back again, so I guess I must have scared them out. That ended my superstitious fear of ghosts to a great extent, and if there was just a bit of it still in my system, the Lord took it out of me when I was saved.

I believe that we sometimes have premonitions or dreams telling us of things to come, but that is not the same as believing in ghosts, and the story I am about to tell you now was, as I see it, a direct message from God. Why God thought so much of a poor, ignorant, lonely boy that He provided a falling star as a message of warning, just when that message was so badly needed and there was no one else to give it, is still beyond my comprehension. Remember that what I am writing down here is not fiction but rather the truth as near as I can remember it, with a little humor thrown in now and then to help drive away the gloom. I will also leave out some things that would implicate others and would not do anyone any good.

Well, Mr. and Mrs. "S" had the custom of going to town every Saturday afternoon to do their trading and the children were in school most of the time, so I was often left alone doing work of some kind around the place. I had made friends with some boys who were pretty tough, and we would meet together once in a while and try to show off, thinking we were rather smart. We had arranged to meet one night in a little place where there was a store to buy cheap cigars and candy and have what we called a good time.

I had no money, but I knew where there was lots of money in the house where I had seen them put it away almost in plain sight, but they always locked the house when they went away. But when the devil gets to talking to a person, he will generally show them the way if they listen to him. So he told me, "You have worked hard around here for a long time, and you are entitled to a little of that money, but don't take too much at first because it might cause suspicion." "Yes, I know," I said, "but how will I get in?"

He said, "Go around to the back of the house. There is a window light right next to the step where the putty has all fallen out and only the little brads hold it in. Pull them out, take out the glass, and reach in. Then pull out the stop, raise the window, and crawl in. Take fifty cents of the money and be sure not to leave any marks anywhere that might cause suspicion. Then put the window light back in just as you found it." And I suppose he might have added, "You will find it easier the next time," but I was too busy planning on keeping my appointment with some of his imps to listen.

You may be skeptical of this being a literal conversation with the devil, but from over sixty years of experience, I know that is just the way he works, and mostly on a small scale to start with. I have God to thank for showing me a better way, which you will learn about if you follow this story to the end. Of course, I took the devil's advice and done just as he told me to, and nobody ever knew a thing about it besides me and the devil.

It so happened that an old-time revival was going on at the schoolhouse and people were being saved. I guess that was one reason Satan was so busy, as he is always on the job at times like that, trying to interfere with God's business. As I started down the road Sunday evening with my stolen treasure, I was anticipating the good time I thought I was going to have spending that fifty cents. Oh yes, a boy of my age who had that much money those days was pretty rich. This time, the straight road led toward Hell, and the crooked narrow road branched off the main road about a quarter of a mile from the house and led to the schoolhouse and the revival meeting.

Now, I had been to Sunday school a few times and had heard the story of Paul's conversion on the road to Damascus, and I began to wonder, *What if such a thing would happen to me?* I slowed up and commenced to think, and the nearer I came to the fork in the road, the slower I went. There seeming to be two powers pulling at me at once. One said go to the church, and the other said meet the boys, they will be expecting you.

As I came to the fork in the road, I stopped and stood there, all of a minute I guess, undecided as to what to do. I had taken only one step onto the main road when all at once, everything became as light as day. It was a dark night, but I could see our old stone house about a quarter mile away, as plainly as if it had been the sunlight of midday. I was scared, you can believe me, as the thing I had been thinking about had really happened, and I felt that God had truly spoken to a poor, lonely, ignorant boy like me. Of course, I went to church, and when I got there, the people were talking about a shooting star they had just seen, and some of the old timers said it was the brightest they had ever seen. I hadn't seen the star, but only the light, and I have never forgotten it and have told this story to many. I suppose the general opinion is that it would have happened anyway, but why did it happen when I was half-expecting something like this to happen?

I went forward during the meeting and had a rather definite experience. But having little help and lots of discouragement, I soon fell back into my old ways except that I never stole anything again from that day to this. And I hope to say something of my real conversion many years later, before I close this life story.

It had been some time since I had seen my brother Elmer, and at Christmas time the community had a

Christmas tree up and was putting on the usual program at the schoolhouse. A good-sized boy sat down behind me and I was not quite sure that it was Elmer in the rather dim light, then he stuck up those stubs of his right hand which settled it immediately. He had caught a ride down with some neighbors, but he had to go back with them, and I did not see him again until I went after him to get him to come out west with me.

There was one winter that we went to another school for some reason, it was about two and a half miles down the river. Most of the river was frozen except for the current, which meandered back and forth across the riverbed. It was quite deep in places, and of course, the ice was very thin where the water ran swiftly. I had gotten a pair of cheap skates in some kind of deal and had learned to skate. Of course, it was easy for me to go to school in the winter, as long as the ice held out. Mr. S's oldest boy also went, and he had no skates, so he would walk, run, and slide along on his overshoes as best he could. This gave me plenty of time to meander around and enjoy myself. He was somewhat younger than I was and was always fooling around near those air holes in the ice. I guess he liked to see the water bubbling and gurgling under the frozen surface. I had told him of the danger, but I guess the spirit of adventure was beginning to bubble up inside him as well.

One evening when we were on our way home, I heard a crash and a splash, accompanied by a loud screech. I looked and there he was, head and shoulders above the ice, and the rest of him below. I made a run for him and somehow managed to pull him out. If it hadn't been for the skates, he would have slipped under the ice, I am sure. He was rather delicate, and I was afraid he would freeze to death before I got him home. It was frigid weather, but by keeping him moving, I managed to get him home before he froze up. But they didn't seem very thankful to me for bringing him home in that condition. Maybe they thought I pushed him. At least I was used to being blamed for mean things I had never done.

Later on, perhaps the next winter, we were on our way to our school when he went into one of his mean streaks and kept kicking me in the shins. I told him if he didn't quit it, I would bash him one, but he thought it was lots of fun to continue those caveman tactics on me. When I had had all I could stand, I lit into him and gave him a good licking. By the time we got to school, he didn't look so good and ran to the teacher to tell her what I had done, failing to tell her what he had done. She asked me if I was ashamed of myself, and I said "No, and if he don't behave himself I'll do it again."

I knew what would happen when I got home, but I had a certain sense of satisfaction, feeling I had got my reward for saving his life. Of course, it is not a very manly thing to do to beat up on one who is smaller than oneself, but I thought the time had come for some measure of correction, and when there was no one else to do it (or willing to do it), I did it myself. Fortunately, he was not hurt much, nor did he kick me around anymore after that.

You will no doubt excuse me if this story is not quite in line, as I will occasionally reach back and bring out some particular happening that I have overlooked, such as the one just related which took place previous to the grain-threshing experience.

I mentioned a cyclone cellar a while back, and of course, when one thinks of Kansas, one thinks of cyclones as well as grasshoppers, hot wind, hailstorms, etc. You no doubt wonder if I was ever in a real cyclone, and the answer is no. I have seen them in action not far away, have seen the damage they can do, and I even holed up in the cellar several times to be safe from them, but thankfully, no cyclone has ever hit a spot where I happened to be.

There was always that great feeling of anticipation every time I saw those fearful-looking clouds that only the Kansas plains' atmosphere can produce. It was very inspiring to see them at a distance; the terrific flashes of lightning and crashes of thunder were wonderful to see and hear out over the plains. I would say I was not afraid of it, but on several occasions the lightning hit so close that it almost knocked me off my feet, and I began to feel that I was not so special after all. So it is with life: that just when we begin to think we are so important and the world could not get along without us, something happens nearby that brings us to realize that there is a power greater than we are, and we had better seek the shelter of His everlasting wings before it is too late.

There are many more tales I could tell about my experiences in Kansas, but I think it's about time we move on to other scenery, perhaps of equal interest. So now, I will explain our preparations for our final exit from the scenes and happenings of my first seventeen years of life.

My father and mother, in the meantime, had built a new home in the city of Denver, Colorado, and my sister Edith had moved out there already, leaving only Elmer and me back in Kansas. My mother wanted us to come out too, but at the same time, I had visions of getting out on my own as a farmer, picturing myself with a nice team, wagon, and harness all my own. But I realized that there was no way to get them without money. So that's how it was, and my vision soon faded, and I sold my saddle pony and decided to go west.

Reunited in Denver

With the money I got from selling my pony, together with a few dollars I had earned on the side, I lit out on foot to see Elmer. It was a fourteen-mile trip, but that was only four or five hours for me in those days, as I could just about match an ordinary horse when it came to getting over the ground in a hurry. I can recall how I felt like I was getting out after a long jail sentence. And there was a great satisfaction in my heart to feel that, and I did not have to hurry back and get home at a certain time. I guess I was thinking of the last time I had visited my brother, and it seemed so nice just to be free for a spell that I stayed over an extra day and got a licking when I got back.

Well, there I was, past seventeen and free, and if you think I did not feel good about it, just try and put yourself in my place. Try to imagine being in bondage, and I think you will be able to form a pretty good idea of just how I felt. Of course, Mr. "S" put up a pretty strong argument for me to stay with him until I was twenty-one, and he said he would fix me up with a good outfit, but I had a suspicion that before the extra four years were up, he would become so disagreeable that I would not be able to stay the extra time and would, therefore, lose my chance for the team and outfit. No, I had made up my mind, and that settled it.

So I went by a little store on the way (or out of the way) and armed myself with fifty cents worth of hard mixed candy, which could be bought then awfully cheap. I used money that was my own, as I always did like candy and sweet things. That was the worst of my vices at that time. As I proceeded on my journey, I ate so much candy that it almost made me sick, as I had no lunch with me. I thought the candy would fill the bill and *me too*, and that I would have plenty left to give Elmer a good feed when I got there.

I had already written Elmer, so our plans were pretty well-decided. We had a good visit, and everything went along fine until the time came to leave, and then he began to weaken, not having the nerve to tell the folks that he was going to leave. I don't know as I blame him much now as I look back on those times, for that had been his home from the time he was a rather small boy. Although the old folks were pretty rough at times, they had also been rather good to him, and it was harder for him to leave than it had been for me. Elmer had a few keepsakes that he valued pretty highly, and he finally decided to get his things together without being seen, and we pulled out to begin the journey. The final preparation for our trip west was not much, for what we had we carried with us.

I had a friend who had gone through something of the same experience we had been through, who was staying with an old couple about three quarters of a mile from the "S" home, and they invited us to spend our last night with them, which we did. I shall never forget our visit there, as these folks were good Christian people, and they had been very good to me. My friend was not a very strong man physically, but he was the most powerful man in prayer that I had ever known. It just seemed that when he prayed, he was talking directly to God, and the power of God came down on the people, as it did in the old-fashioned Methodist camp meetings or revivals where people were saved. Well, I think it would be a good thing if we had more of those people who knew how to pray these days, and not so many religious bosses and warmongers.

Before we went to bed that night, he called us together and read from the Bible. Then we all knelt, and he prayed for the two boys who were going out into a strange world, to meet strange people, and to be subject to all manner of temptation. And he prayed that God would watch over us and save us, in the end, for His glory. Well, that was about fifty-seven years ago and I have never forgotten that prayer, and I am sure that God never forgot it either because I was finally and definitely saved about thirty years ago. There may have been a period of perhaps twenty-five to thirty years between John Kidd's wonderful prayer and my real conversion that I may have lived an ungodly life. If so, it was not John's fault or God's fault, but my own, for I became careless and forgot there was a God and was nothing more than a lost sinner for all those many years.

Elmer and I started out that morning on our own, stopping long enough at the "S" place to get my few things together and tie them in a little bundle and bid goodbye to Mrs. "S" (Mr. "S" was away somewhere). As we looked back from the top of a little hill on the road, we saw for the last time the old stone house that Father had built. Although it had been enlarged and improved, there stood the same old stonewalls, storing up the morning sunshine that had sheltered us when we were little boys together. No doubt, they are still standing there as a lasting memorial to the efforts of the early Kansas settlers. A little over a half mile to the north was the old schoolhouse where I received about the only education I ever got (I had just started the sixth grade).

After a final look at the "S" farm and all the familiar scenes spread out before me, there came over me such a feeling of utter loneliness that I almost lost heart. Well, fifteen years of a boy's life seems a long time, and no matter how hard and discouraging those fifteen years had been, back there along old "Skunk Creek" and along the banks of the old Solomon River, there were many places (and some people) that held very pleasant memories for me. There was the old swimming hole, the good fishing spots along the river, and the old cottonwood grove where Elmer had met with his accident and where we used to climb to the topmost branches of the large trees. We were saying goodbye forever, not only to the places and people, but to our boyhood days as well, and as we turned our back to it all and went on our way, our hearts were not so light as they had been at the thought of being free in the first place. I had not completely recovered when we passed the cemetery on the road to town, for there, sleeping and awaiting the call of the Great Judge, was my girlfriend and boyhood sweetheart, who had died of diphtheria when old Doc Landon had been called too late.

We continued on and soon found ourselves in the little town of Marvin, just four miles from our old home. We shopped around a little and then proceeded on to the place where Edith had lived for several years with a family by the name of Daum. They were fine people and treated us well, and we stayed all night with them. They had a nice farm, and Mr. Daum told me if I didn't like it in Denver to come back and he would give me a job the whole year round and pay me ten dollars a month plus board, which were good wages in those days. It beat board and clothes anyway. I was just about half in the notion to stay, but the urge to see the Great City got the upper hand.

The next day, Mr. "D" took us to Phillipsburg where they helped us out with buying some new clothes and other things we would need. Then they went with us to buy our tickets for Denver. We were a pretty badly excited pair of boys and as green as was possible for a person to be, never having ridden on a train or even been out of the country in which we had grown up. Mr. "D" did not stay to see us off, as he had his chores to attend to, and the train did not leave until 8:45 p.m., so we were left to our own resources, which were mighty limited since this was all new to us.

If we had just watched the other fellows and did what they did, it might have been all right, but we had to show our ignorance by doing things our own way. We got on the train somehow and got in our seats, and after a while the conductor came along and asked for our tickets. After he had operated on them with some kind of machine that we had never seen before, he gave us each a piece of cardboard in exchange for the largest portion of our tickets and told us to put it in our hats.

We had our hats on our laps, as we wished to be polite, and had removed them when we got on the train, so we turned our hats top down and proceeded to do what he had told us to do. We surely watched those cardboard tickets closely, fearing that some thief might come along and steal them. Then we looked around and happened to see how the tickets were placed in the men's hatbands! Feeling silly, I did likewise, wondering how many had laughed at our ignorance.

Well, we sat all night watching the sparks go by the windows and listened to the car wheels click over the joints in the rails, never sleeping a wink. We just waited and watched for the first streak of dawn so we could see something of the kind of country we were going through. Morning came at last, and as we looked out to the southwest, we saw what we thought was a big blue cloud with a white top, and we were watching it intently when the newsboy came along and asked, "Do you see Pike's Peak?" I thought he was just kidding us, for I had thought of Pike's Peak as a very sharp peak, rearing up into the sky with hardly any mountains around it. But as it grew lighter, we began to see the great snow-capped range of the Rocky Mountains, and to us two boys who had never seen anything but a small chalk hill, it was the most inspiring sight we had ever seen.

When we left Colorado Springs and turned north, the snow-capped range of mountains was visible as far as the eye could see, and when we arrived in Denver we still could not see the end of them. It was April, and anyone who has never seen the Rockies from where we saw them cannot fully appreciate the wonder of it all. It was to be many years before we would leave the everlasting sight of the Rocky Mountains. Between the years of 1888 and 1910, I believe I was out of sight of them only once or twice. They became more familiar (and were friendlier to me) than the Kansas plains.

When our train was within a few miles of Denver, we began getting a little nervous, like most greenhorns do, wondering whether our sister Edith would be there at the depot to greet us. When the conductor came along and asked if there was anyone waiting for us, we told him that our sister was supposed to be there, but we were not sure if she got our letter. He said that if she did not show up, to wait in the waiting room until he came around, and he would see to it that we got on the right streetcar to get to our destination.

I will always remember the kindness of that conductor, for he knew we were a pair of "hayseeds" who knew nothing of the ways of a great city. He was enough interested in us to look out for our welfare. This good man had no idea his kind offer would still be remembered and mentioned by one of those boys, when that boy had grown old and gray, and in his eyes, this would probably have been ample reward for his small offer of kindness. But Edith was there to meet us at the depot, and we were very glad. Although I will venture to say she must have been somewhat embarrassed piloting two "hayseeds" around the crowded city. Somehow, she managed to get us to the streetcar and out to our parents' home.

I will not attempt to give you a picture of our meeting after so many years. It is sufficient to say we were all very glad to see each other again. Mother and Father and my two sisters were there, but Aaron was out in the mountains somewhere. No one knew where he was at the time. He was quite a wanderer and would disappear for months at a time, not telling the folks where he was. Then he would show up again unannounced. We were at home quite a while before he returned.

We naturally had some rather embarrassing experiences before we got initiated into the ways of city life but soon caught on pretty well. Still, I don't think I ever took on the polish like some people do, for I had been in God's outdoors so many years that I did not feel entirely at home in the city.

My first job was digging up six city lots for a dollar a day, and I finished the job in record time, feeling pretty rich when I went home with those big silver cartwheels jingling in my pocket. Then I took a job cleaning brick, making about a dollar a day until the job was finished. As I have said before, Father was a carpenter and was working for a building contractor. I think he must have worked for this man for over thirty years. He got me my next job as an apprentice, learning the carpenter trade.

Early in my apprenticeship, we were working on a house about twenty miles out of town, a small-frame building. After we had the frame up, we discovered that one corner was a little low, so they put some prys under it to lift it up and had me to do the blocking up, and suddenly the two-by-fours we were using broke. The weight of the building came down and caught my thumb, mashing it flat. They fixed me up the best they could and sent me home over twenty miles away. I had no money with me and was too bashful to ask for any, so I started off walking toward home, my arm in a sling, not feeling too good. I had to walk the entire distance, and since it was about two-thirty in the afternoon when I struck out, I was forced to walk all the way through a strange city after dark. I do not know how I kept from getting lost, but God remembers the strangers and provides an instinct, sometimes, that leads one better than sight does. That was the end of my building job, and it was some little while before I got another steady job, working in a planing mill and cleaning up shop at seventy-five cents for a ten-hour day.

One Sunday morning, Elmer and I thought it would be a good stunt and a fine way to spend the Sabbath if we were to take a little walk out into the mountains to do a little exploring and maybe some prospecting. Not even taking a lunch, we started out, feeling in good spirits and thinking we would soon be there since the mountains looked so close in the morning sunshine. After walking about two hours, we could see they still were still a long way off and began to wonder why we were not making better headway. We put on a little extra steam but still did not seem to be gaining on them very much. We could not turn back now, so on we trudged until the long shadows of the nearer foothills commenced to come out toward us.

When we finally reached the bottom of what we thought were the mountains, it was getting pretty late in the day. Not wanting to give up yet, we climbed to the top of one hill, only to discover that there was a long drop and then another hill that was very much higher than the one we had just climbed. This must be it, we thought, so on we went to the top of the second hill, and behold, still another and then another higher one. We just looked for a while, in wonder, and then turned back like Lot's wife, casting our eyes out over the plains below us. There in the distance, we saw the city of Denver in the late evening sunlight, and it looked very small and a long ways off.

We were sore, tired, and hungry, so we were very thankful that most of the way back was downhill. We began our descent, and before we had left the lower foothills, the lights of the city could be plainly seen. From then on, I guess we just went by the glitter of those lights, as there was not even a trail to follow, and when we finally got home, it was about ten o'clock. Of course, by then we were completely worn-out and almost starved. When we told the folks what we had done, Dad had a good laugh. Well, they say Denver is about sixteen miles from the mountains, or foothills rather, so you can guess how far we hiked that day. Since then, I have learned something about distances in the mountains, and that was my first lesson.

Denver at that time was in a great boom. This was about the time of the big gold strikes at Cripple Creek and other mining fields, and there was a great surplus population there. It was sometimes a hard job to get through the foot traffic because there were no such things as automobiles then, and very few bikes or electric streetcars either. There was just one cable car line, the rest of the streetcars being drawn by horses. All the money was either gold or silver, and there was lots of it in circulation, but very little of it circulated my way. I was just an ignorant country kid, not schooled in the ways of the world. If some of the workers of our time who are unsatisfied with ten or twelve dollars a day were forced to work for a while at the wages paid back then, they would truly have something to strike for.

I was as large as a man at this time, and I worked for nearly a year, putting in ten-hour days for four dollars and fifty cents a week. I paid over half of that for board. So you see, I didn't have much to sport around on. The first pair of shoes I remember buying cost me a dollar and twenty-five cents. But I still managed to buy my clothes, pay my board, and go to a show once in a while before getting a raise in my pay. Then I bought one of those old-fashioned bicycles with the big wheel in front and a little wheel behind, and that became a source of recreation, expense, and hard falls for the next year or so. Then, about the time I got it paid for, I traded in the wreck and got a little better one. I could save carfare by gearing up my own means of navigation to a pair of wheels, and that saved me sixty cents a week, which was something for those times.

About this time, Aaron came back to Denver and had to have one of those things (a bicycle of his own). His was more up-to-date and had wheels of equal size. It was known as a "safety bike" at the time because a person did not have so far to fall when he lost his balance. We used to spend about all of our surplus energy making trips out to the little towns within a radius of twenty miles or so, on Sundays or holidays. I am sure that was better than hanging around in pool halls, gambling joints, or saloons, of which there were plenty in Denver.

On several occasions, we joined up with the bicycle club, and we all went out together, seventy or eighty of us. One Sunday we rode to Greeley, about fifty-seven miles down the Platte River, and then we all had dinner there at the hotel. Only a few of us rode our wheels back to Denver, while the rest took the train, and those of us still riding stopped at the creamery and filled up on buttermilk. It was a very hot day, and we were pretty thirsty, so we drank too much and got sick, and still had to peddle our way back under the influence of too much buttermilk. If seasickness is any worse, I do not care to go on a boat journey. We figured that when we got home that evening, we had traveled about 125 miles under our own power, and only used about one gallon of buttermilk. That was pretty cheap transportation, considering the buttermilk was free.

One time, we went out with the bicycle club to a little town called Brighton. There was only one of the new type of low-wheel bicycles in the bunch, and the boys joshed the rider all the way down about the freak he was riding. By about the next year, it was reversed. There was only one high-wheel (so they said), and he got the kidding. That was about how long it took to change that mode of wheel transportation back then. Now, over fifty years later, there has been little change in the style of the safety bicycle, except that they have put a gas motor on some of them, and they use gasoline instead of buttermilk and knee action.

I had been working in the planing mill several months, and one Sunday I thought I would go out to one of the summer resorts and spend the day there. The streetcar company was putting on some special doings to attract the public and, perhaps, offering a little cut in rates. I made my way out there and mooned around seeing the sights until it was getting pretty late in the evening, and so I thought it was about time to head home.

I went up to the car terminal, and there was such a mob of people of the same mind (as I) that I had to just grab on wherever I could get a handhold. The car was one of those of the style that had open sides with a long step running the full length of the car, and as the seats had all been taken, there were a lot of us just hanging onto the side of the car. The engineer, when pulling into the coal shed, failed to uncouple the engine from the car, and I was caught between the car and the side of the building. When this happened, I was pretty badly crushed through the hips and I fell off in a heap.

Although Mother and Father were on the car, I did not know where they were. I guess I must have let out a pretty loud yell because Mother recognized my voice and I was surprised and glad. Well, somehow, they got me home and to the doctor, and he said it was just a bad sprain and that there were no bones broken, but I was laid up for about three months. The company paid me a hundred dollars, and I gave Mother fifty, the doc thirty-five, and had fifteen left over. After three months, most of the time on crutches, I went back to work again, but according to the wages I was getting and barring the doctor bill, I didn't lose much money in the deal. Still, it was several years before I completely recovered.

On another occasion, I went out to one of those resorts to see a man fly, so we thought, and when we got out there, it looked like the whole city had turned out to see this unheard-of stunt. It had been well-advertised, but all we saw were two high posts set in the ground with a wire stretched across from one to the other, and this great mob of people looking on. Well, pretty soon, what seemed to be a huge many-colored bird came out of a side door of a building and made its way to the nearest post. Then a man came along and fastened a hook that was suspended from a pulley on the wire to a kind of a harness on the birdman's back. The idea, so it seems, was for him to work his way from one post to the other by using a pair of wings that were fastened onto him somehow. About this time, rocks and different kinds of missiles commenced to fly through the air, and our birdman had to hunt for his nest or he would have been mobbed. That was before the days of the Wright brothers, and men had never been known to fly with a heavier-than-air machine. People naturally were curious to see the first man to fly and were angry when they were fooled in that way, and who could blame them?

When we think of what has been accomplished along that line since that time, we wonder what is next. We are horrified to think of what those machines of the air have been used for and will continue to be used for, unless God intervenes and changes men's hearts. Perhaps, someday they will be used for the benefit of mankind rather than for his destruction.

This was about the time of the balloon fad, and men were going up in hot-air balloons and dropping out with parachutes. We three boys used to go up on a hill and watch them with a very good large telescope that Aaron had bought at a second-hand shop. There was an old white-whiskered man by the name of King, who made balloon ascensions at Sloan's Lake Resort, and he used gas instead of hot air in his balloons. One day, they had advertised that there would be a young couple getting married in the balloon and then making their honeymoon trip in the air, so we boys went out to our observation point and watched the balloons go up. He had put a small balloon on the side to help carry the extra weight, and the balloon and its passengers sailed right up into a thunderstorm and were quickly out of sight in the clouds. Not for long, though, for they soon came back in sight with the top of the big balloon covered with snow and flapping around in the wind like a loose tent. It had been hit by lightning and was coming down fast. It gradually took on the shape of a huge parachute, which was the only thing that saved the lives of the honeymooners and the pilot. It sure came down fast, but the small balloon and the big balloon formed a good enough parachute, so it broke the fall, and they were not badly hurt.

I suppose we were a fairly good average of young American patriotism when the Fourth of July came around, and perhaps a little more so when it came to making a big noise. As cannon for firecrackers and torpedoes cost quite a bit, and there seemed to be certain limits to the size and booming capacity for this brand of fireworks, we commenced to exercise our inventive qualities to figure out something else that would be cheap and still fit the bill. So we laid in a good supply of black powder and got busy. First, we found an old shotgun barrel, loaded it up, and set it off. But it blew up and sailed away with the greatest of ease. So I found a piece of heavy one-and-a-half inch water pipe, about three feet long, and drilled a small hole in the center of it to insert the fuse. We put a good charge of powder in it, packed plenty of paper in from both ends, and set it off. Well, the results were just what we were looking for but very annoying to the neighbors, as it was enough to jar the earth.

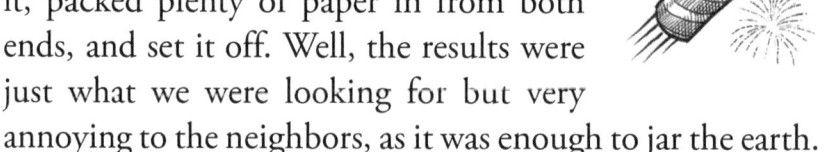

We kept it up at intervals until almost twelve o'clock, when we thought it a good idea to give her an extra good charge and let it off, just at midnight, as a farewell shot. It proved to be just that to the old gas pipe, for we never saw it again, although we searched all over the neighborhood for it. Eventually, we went up an alley, found a man stretched out across the ground, and thought we had killed him! We were pretty badly scared until we smelt the whiskey, and that was one time when whiskey really smelt good. We recognized old Dutch Fred, the neighborhood drunk, and since we knew where he lived, we picked him up, carried him up a flight of stairs, and put him to bed. We were sure glad he was only dead drunk, and also glad that we had ended the night of noise-making with a good deed, which was some restitution for the misery we had caused others that day. But please don't try to duplicate our method of celebrating the fourth of July. It might backfire and hurt someone, and we were surely old enough to have known better.

The part of town where my folks had bought their building lot had been an old cemetery, and in removing the bodies, they had missed one here and there. When Father had gotten his cellar part way dug, he found what remained of a six-foot tall man. Father had been unsuccessful in getting the proper authorities to remove him, so the body was still there when we came to Denver. Mother had not been able to shake off the old superstitious training of her girlhood days, and she was rather uneasy about the underground inhabitant who had not quite yet made it back to the earth from which he came. I didn't feel so good about it myself at first, but it didn't seem to bother Dad any as he was an old war veteran and had laid down and slept among the dead on the battlefield. He did not intend to let this one scare him out, but Mother was to be reckoned with, and the man was finally removed.

I was the official fire builder, as I have been for most of my life, and right by the kitchen stove was a small window. It was my custom, after I had lit the fire, to look out the window to see what the weather was like. This window afforded a good view of our neighbor's backyard and the dirt walk around their house, just a hard-beaten path almost directly under our window. Well, it had been raining for several days, and as I looked out the window this particular morning, right in the middle of the path was a hole, maybe two and a half by five feet, that had sunken down about ten or twelve inches during the night. For a while, I wondered what it was all about, but then I remembered the old fellow in the cellar. My first impulse was to go over and tell our neighbor about it, as she was a nervous woman, and it was her custom to come out around the house about this time in the morning. But Satan said to me, "She was the one who raised such a fuss about your Fourth of July racket, so why not watch the fun?" Well, it soon happened. Out she came, walking very fast, and did not see the thing until she was very close to it, then she threw up her hands and looked like she would faint.

It has been said that revenge is sweet, but I have long since learned that it is very much the opposite. I have never been proud of this stunt, for she was a very good woman and was only being a good citizen when she objected to our disruption of the peace in the community. I guess the main reason for us feeling as we did toward her was that my mother was always doing things for her that we thought she should do for herself, such as washing her clothes.

On one occasion, I got a small jigsaw, and to practice up, I found a piece of an old soapbox that had printed on it "Bath, Toilet and Laundry" in big letters. I started to operate on it with my jigsaw and then cut out the word *laundry*. I was successful to such an extent that I thought it too good to waste, so I took the opportunity when our lady friend was away one day to tack it up on her front porch where it could be seen from the street. She soon had quite a number of callers waiting to have their laundry done! But she took this in a good, sportsmanlike manner, and both she and her husband had a good laugh out of it, which was okay. This good woman and her husband, who proved to be a good friend of mine later on, have long since gone to their great reward, where there are no would-be toughs to bother them.

I remember when the patent medicine shows came to town selling Indian (what they called Indian) remedies. One was called Chickasaw Indian Sagwa, and another was called Kickapoo Indian Pulkee, and they set up their camps on a vacant block, not far from where we lived. They had a bunch of Indians doing the war dance and other Indian stunts and put on quite a free show. At intervals of about an hour or so, a man who had all the tone of a circus announcer would get up on a stand and tell of all the healing qualities these medicines possessed, while demonstrating it by making their application to some old cripple who would volunteer from the audience after having been hired and trained, of course, for the demonstration.

After they had rubbed a little on his supposed-to-be crippled body or given him a dose inwardly, he would suddenly recover from his ailment and proceed to demonstrate that the dope was just as good or better than advertised. And it usually sold for a dollar a bottle, I suppose so it would not take much time to make change, and there was no "nuisance tax" in those days. Well, the way the people would gobble up this supposed healer of life, you would think they were afraid there would not be enough to go around, although it was only a short ways to the irrigation ditch.

My younger sister, Cora, was about thirteen or fourteen at that time and always ready to make a lot of commotion, so she learned from the Indians how to dance the Indian war dance as well as do the Indian chant and beat the drum. When she armed herself with an old dishpan and something to pound it with, like an old hatchet, and had stuck a few feathers in her black hair, you would have thought the Sioux tribe had gone on the warpath again. Those were happy days for my younger sister, and it is a good thing they were, for she was soon to learn the stern realities of life after getting married to a whiskey bum at the early age of sixteen. From that time on, she was to know many heartaching experiences, so I am glad she had a happy girlhood. But this is my story, and if I get off on too many side roads, I will never get it told.

Cora Slothower, Robert's little sister at about age fifteen. Taken in Denver, CO circa 1890

As I sit in my Washington home today, trying to exert my memory to recall the highlights of my lifetime's experiences, I find it rather hard to pick out the things that would be most interesting. But now an experience involving a turkey and my wheel comes to mind. When Christmas time came around one year, while I still had my old high bicycle, the lumber company I worked for gave each married man a turkey, and the single men a dollar and fifty cents, which would just about equal the price of a turkey in those days. I told the man who had charge of handing out the turkeys that I had a large family, which was true, as there were seven in our family at that time. Although I was not married, he saved out a twenty-pound turkey for me and I had to get that thing home. It was about three miles away, through the town and after nightfall, and I put the turkey on the wheel and tried to hold onto it while I walked and pushed the two of them the three miles.

Several times during this rather strenuous trip, the turkey got both me and the wheel down on the ground, but by the sheer strength of willpower and perseverance, I finally got home by about ten o'clock, not having had my supper yet. Then Mother informed me that she had bought a turkey already and that she didn't have a bake pan large enough to roast my turkey in, so I had to go to the hardware store the next morning and buy a pan big enough for the turkey. Well, I always felt that I had contributed my share toward that Christmas dinner, and to the best of my recollection, that was the last Christmas dinner our family ever had together with all of us present. Fate had so ordered that we were soon to separate again, though we visited home once in a while. Our interests or lots were to be cast somewhere else as far as we three boys were concerned.

Elmer and I had been working in the planing mill over two years, and I had been promoted to a job at the bench learning the carpenter trade at much better wages. At about this time, Aaron suggested that I get a layoff for a couple of weeks and go with him on our bikes out into Wyoming. Aaron had spent some time on a previous trip and knew a number of people who were ranchers out there. So I got my layoff and we started out one morning on our two hundred-and-fifty mile trip.

We had quite an experience, my brother having the bad luck to break his wheel down the first day out. We could not find anyone who could fix it, so we had a long hike and got caught in a rainstorm, getting wet, cold, and hungry. We finally found shelter and food with a very kind-hearted farmer near Greeley. The next morning, we pushed our wheels several miles to a little town and tried to get his wheel fixed at a blacksmith shop. They said they could not fix it, but Aaron asked the blacksmith if he would let him dig into the junk pile, and after getting his consent, Aaron found what he needed and soon had the wheel fixed. That was where his mechanical ideas came in pretty handy again, and that is the one and only time that I ever knew him to take a glass of beer or any other intoxicating drink. I guess he felt so good about the bike that he wanted to celebrate. We were soon on our way again and very happy.

We were three days getting to Cheyenne, riding many miles over roads that were nothing but ruts between an almost solid bed of cactus which later became one of the garden spots of Colorado. The wheels we were riding then did not use inflated tires, so the spines of the cactus caused us very little worry. The trip from Cheyenne to the summit of the mountains was a long hard climb, and as we stopped to view the monument, I lost control of my wheel and took a bad header. This was to remind me that everything that goes up must come down, and getting on top of the Rockies for the first time was no exception to the rule. The wheeling now was very much easier and we were soon in Laramie, having ridden sixty miles over the top of the mountains.

Another three days and we were out in the hills where Aaron had built a cabin. He had a bad headache most of the day, and he said if he could get a good shot of sagebrush tea, he would be all right, as he thought sagebrush tea was a cure-all. There was an old stove in the cabin, and we soon had a fire going. We found a tin can for the tea, and I supposed I was going to get something pretty good, but when I took a swig of it, it nearly knocked me over because it was so bitter. Well, I was to live many years among the sagebrush, clearing and grubbing out over one hundred acres of it, but I never learned to like sagebrush tea and could never bring myself to believe it done a sick person any good.

I will not dwell on this ranch scene out there in the hills, as I was to spend many years of my life within a mile or so of Aaron's old log cabin. His place sat in the hills at the north end of the great Laramie plains at an altitude of over seven thousand feet above sea level. For a few days, I stayed at a ranch Aaron was figuring on buying, and then I mounted my wheel and rode to Rock Creek, about twenty-seven miles away. From there, I took the train back to Denver and my job, checking my wheel and sitting back in the cushions and taking it easy, while Aaron stayed on at the ranch.

It was agreed that Elmer and I was to work until the next spring, save our money, and then both go back out there and start in the ranching business together, which we did.

I will never forget that trip out to the ranch in April of 1892. When we got off the train at Rock Creek it was snowing like crazy. Aaron was there to meet us with the team, and the next morning the ground was covered with several inches of snow, and the sun was shining bright. We loaded up our things and a wagonload of supplies and started out over the twenty-seven miles of snow-covered plains, without a house to be seen along the road. Of course, we had been working inside all winter, and the bright sun shining down on the snow was pretty tough on our eyes. The horses began to tire with this heavy lugging, and by the time we had gotten over what was called Pine Ridge, they were pretty well tired out. Although we had stopped a while for rest at about noontime, we were in the same fix as the horses, as we had walked just about all the way in order to lighten the load on them.

When we got within about three miles of our destination, the team was just about all in, so we unhitched them, gave them a feed of oats and a drink of water at the stream, and built a fire with some sagebrush. We made some coffee and had some lunch and rested for a while before continuing on our journey, which was all uphill from there on.

It was twelve at night when we pulled in at the ranch, and we were a very weary bunch, except for Aaron, who was pretty well hardened up from his hiking all around. If he was tired, he never said a thing about it, but that was his way. Well, when we got up the next morning and tried to look out on our new surroundings, I could not see, as my eyes felt as if there was a red-hot iron being stuck in them every time I tried to open them. For several days, I was just about blind. Elmer was not so bad off as I was. I guess his eyes were stronger than mine. And such was the beginning of the Slothower brothers' ranching experience.

We were going to raise hay, grain, and potatoes and sell the products of the ranch, but no livestock as Aaron did not like to handle stock. Being the oldest, he was supposed to be the boss. It was a very pretty place there, surrounded by mountains on all sides, with a creek running through the center of a small valley. There were meadows on both sides of the creek and irrigation ditches to irrigate the meadows. I fancy I can still hear the roaring of the mountain stream as it meandered its way over the rocks. Especially in the spring and early summer when the snow was melting. It was music to my lonely soul.

At times, there was not much else to listen to besides the howling of the coyote or the long-drawn-out mournful howl of the wolf and the call of the night birds coming from the surrounding hills. These familiar sounds of the night serve to remind us that the world is not all dead or asleep when there are no human voices to be heard. I could never fully understand the charm of the mountains, which will sometimes hold one in their spell and sometimes drive away the terrible loneliness, even when there is not a human being within miles. All those things I was to learn later in my many years of experience in these same hills. I will tell more about them at a time still in the future, assuming there is no "providential hindrance." At this time, this rather brief description will suffice, for I was to stay there only one year for reasons I will not mention here. We put up the hay, bailed it, and then spent the greater part of that winter hauling it over the long hard road I have already mentioned and getting very little for the hay.

There was one experience I will tell about that nearly cost us our lives. One very cold morning, Aaron and I started out with a four-horse and a two-horse team and a trail wagon. Out there in the hills, there was very little fresh snow, but when we got out on the plains, the snow commenced to get deeper. The farther we went, the deeper it got. When we got to within seven miles of our destination, our horses gave out, and we had to stop for the night. There was about six to eight inches of new snow, and there had been no wind since it fell, which was something very unusual on those open plains. I say open because there was not an obstruction sufficient to check the wind—in the direction from which the prevailing winds blew—for over fifty miles. We were afraid the wind would start to blow, so we unhitched our horses, fed and watered them (there being a spring there), and tied them to the trail wagon, which we had unloaded.

We took bales of hay and built up a windbreak on three sides, leaving it open to the east, and stretched a blanket over the top, with bales of hay to hold it down, then put our bed inside as we always carried a heavy roll of bedding. Then after we had broken up one of the feed boxes to build a fire, we made some coffee and rolled into bed. You may be sure that I did not sleep much, just lying there listening for the first sound of wind, which I was almost certain would come. I did not have to wait long, for there was soon a howling blizzard around us, and I thought of those poor horses tied out there to the wagon. We did not dare to throw our covers off until we knew it was daylight, so we could see. We waited hours until we were sure it was light enough and then pushed the covers back, the snow rolling in all around us. Our shelter had drifted full of snow, which was the only thing that saved our lives. Later, when we finally got into town, they said that the temperature had fallen to forty-three degrees below zero that morning. How we ever harnessed up those six horses, loaded the hay, hitched up, and pulled out of that blizzard without freezing to death, I do not know.

When we got within about three miles of town, we met a man by the name of Matheson who had a team and wagon and was coming out to haul in "the frozen Slothowers," but the Slothowers more than met him halfway. The people in town knew we were on the way because a party had passed us the day before and saw us going in with just a light wagon.

About this man, Matheson, I will tell more at a later date. I think it is sufficient here to say that he always seemed to somehow appear when people were in trouble. And I will say, I have lived in communities claiming further advancement in Christian civilization that did not produce many such characters as old Bill Matheson. I am not backward in giving his real name here, and I believe the Lord will remember it up there. We laid over that night in town, heading back to the hills the following day. As sometimes happens, the cold winds turned into a Chinook, and before we got home, the roads had become wet and slippery in places. One thing that made the homecoming end of the journey a great pleasure was the big pot of hot stew that Elmer generally had cooked up for us. It usually consisted of antelope meat, potatoes, onions, "rutabagers" and just about everything else the ranch had produced, and some canned goods thrown in for good measure.

After that winter, I decided that there was not enough profit in the ranch business for all three of us, so I turned my interests over to the other two boys and went back to Denver and to my old job again at better pay than when I had left. Things went along fine, and I saved up some money and made a payment on an almost-new bicycle. But it seemed things were too good to last, for that was the spring of 1893, which most old-timers remember as the "Coxey's Army year" and the year of the great panic.

The mill commenced to lay men off, first a few at a time, and then in larger lots until it came to my turn, after which there were only a few men left at the mill. The boss told me that he thought it would not last long, so I left my tools there and went back every few days, hoping to get back on the job again. But the panic held on through the summer and into the next winter, and I never went back. And so ended my hopes of becoming a cabinetmaker. It also changed the course of my whole life. I will not go into minor details, or tell of the many things that happened during the next year, as it is sufficient to say that I done a lot of going from place to place, looking for something to do, and trying to get enough money so that I would not be too much of a burden to anyone. I still had my wheel, even though I still owed money on it, but they let me keep it, believing as I did, that I would get a job and finish paying for it. So I made several trips out into the country, sometimes looking for work and sometimes just looking to pass the time and see different places. It did not cost much money, just plenty of leg exercise, which was much better for me than bumming around town.

I had a young friend who had lost his job around the same time that I had, a Swede I will call Alek. He had been in the United States just long enough to become pretty well Americanized. He had a good bike, so we made up our minds to go panning for gold up in Clear Creek Canyon, twenty miles or so west of Denver. We got a shovel and a gold pan and started out one morning with our riding britches on. We wore knee pants when riding, with an extra pair of long pants tied to the handlebars. When we got to a place called Golden, we laid in a supply of what we thought we would need in the grocery line, then wheeled on up the Canyon several miles to where we thought there to be plenty of gold, according to some old miners' stories we had heard. We parked our wheels and made our way through brush and rocks—until we found a suitable place to work—and got busy with the shovel and gold pan, taking turns at it. I had done a little placer mining, but Alek was new at the game. He soon caught on.

We got some very fine colors of gold all right, but we figured that at the rate at which it was turning out, we wouldn't be able to make a fortune very soon. So we went back to our wheels and found a suitable place to make a little fire and eat our lunch, and though it was getting dark, we found the soft side of a boulder and bedded down for the night. With nothing under us but the earth and nothing over us but the stars, we nearly froze. Needless to say, we did not sleep very much that night, and when at last the bright sun shone down into that old canyon, it sure felt good to our cold, weary bodies.

Clear Creek is a very rapid mountain stream, and the roaring of the water over the rocks is terrific. There was a narrow-gage railroad running up the canyon that was just about as crooked as the creek, and owing to the noise of the water, a person could not hear the train until it was very close. For some distance, we had to use the right-of-way to get to where we had stopped for the night. We discovered that hanging over the rocks in great clusters were the finest chokecherries I had ever seen, just about ripe. At once, I got to thinking of the Kansas chokecherries and of the time when I had eaten too many and had gotten a bad spell of the *cholera morbus*, and I wondered if these would have the same effect. I ate some of them and proceeded to test them out, but my former experience had taught me a lesson, so I did not eat too many. But I thought, *What a pity for all of them to go to waste, they would make good jelly, and Mother would appreciate some of them for that purpose.*

How to carry them home was the problem until I hit upon the idea of tying the bottom of the legs of my extra pair of pants together, filling them up with chokecherries, and then tying them on the handlebars of the bike. We had plenty of gold, such as it was, to last us for some time, and especially plenty of the cold night mountain air. So we packed up as we were, with the pair of pants stuffed with cherries and a gold pan strapped over my shoulders. Alek carried the shovel over his shoulder, and we hit the trail back.

Well, when we got onto the main road, it was all downhill and easygoing, and we were into Denver in a short while. As we crossed the city, we sure got plenty of guying from the kids, but we finally got home. When I unloaded the chokecherries, I expected Mother to be greatly pleased, but she gave all the cherries to the neighbors.

I had another friend who was a cigar maker, and he had a brother who had an interest in a boating business in Grand Lake, Colorado. He wanted me to go with him on a trip up there where we could go fishing and pass the time for a week or so. So we bought our tickets to Georgetown, Colorado, checked our wheels and rode the train over the same steep, crooked road up the Canyon where Alek and I had had our experience. I remembered the chokecherries, and when we got to that location, I raised the window and, when the opportunity arose, reached out to the overhanging rocks and grabbed a few bunches as the train toiled along up the steep grade. They wondered where I got the fruit, and it is needless to say that was the only time I ever picked fruit from a moving passenger coach.

When we got to Georgetown, we got our wheels and started out to cross the Berthoud Pass into Middle Park. The road was so steep, we had to push our wheels just about all the way to the top of the pass, which is 11,500 feet above sea level. There we were, at the edge of the timberline, and within a stone's throw of snow on the twenty-seventh of August. As we stood there, it seemed that we were nearly on top of the world. We just looked and wondered, while we rested up a while before continuing the journey. I will mention this friend's name here, as we were to meet again on several occasions, and Ed Apple proved himself to be a friend when I so badly needed one years later. We rode the same make of bikes, and we had climbed almost to the top of the Rockies by pushing them ahead of us at a very much higher place than where Aaron and I had crossed at Sherman's Hill. Our wheels were to stand us in good stead for the rest of the trip and it was downhill and on the level most of the way from there on.

It was getting late now, and it would be out of the question for us to make it to the lake that night, so we stopped by a mountain stream that had its source in the everlasting snow that was just above us. As we got down on the rocks to drink, a mountain trout splashed water in my face, and if fish could laugh, I'll bet he had a good laugh at me. After leaving the top of the pass, we traveled several miles down a steep hill and then stopped for the night. As it was, there was a clearing and there was no danger of the fire getting away, so we built up a good fire and spent the night there with the same bedding and covering we had used the night Alek was with me on the placer mining trip. Then we rode on to the lake the next day.

Grand Lake is a very pretty lake, with mountains rising from all sides, except where the Grand River flows out to the south. The water was very clear at the time I was there in August 1893. There was an abundance of lake trout, and in the morning and evening, by using artificial flies, in a short time one could catch all the trout one could use. We had a free boat, and I ate so many trout that I thought they would never taste good again, as bread and fish were about all we ate. There was an old ghost town there that they said had been a hideout for a gang of outlaws in times past and was just about deserted at the time I was there. It was a very nice place to spend a vacation, and there were some tourists there at that time. I was restless as I have always been when not busy, and after a week there, I left my friend and started back alone.

After a hard day's riding I came out on top of the hills almost in sight of Denver, and laid out there in the cold another night. This was not so very far from the place where Alek and I had had our mining experience. When I got into town, it was the same old restless place with hundreds of people parading the streets with nothing to do but get into mischief. I was sorry I had not stayed longer out in the silent hills, where there was at least peace, and rest from the noise and confusion of dissatisfied people.

While at an outdoor meeting one night, where Coxey's army was getting ready to go to Washington, I met a fellow who had a new Cleveland bicycle like mine. As we were each praising the good qualities of our mounts, I found out that he was out of a job—like I was. As misery likes company, we decided to make a trip out to the ranch in Wyoming the next morning. We started out together, but after two days of hard riding, he gave up, so I went on alone. After helping the boys out a little, I got uneasy again and started back on my trip of 250 miles, hoping that things would open up and I could go to work.

I had made it back as far as Loveland, Colorado, and when I got up the next morning, the newsboy was telling about a lynching in Denver. I bought a paper and read about a mob tearing out the side of the city jail, taking an Italian out and hanging him from a tree in the jail yard, and then shooting him full of holes. They then dragged him through the streets and hung his body from a lamppost in front of the news office. All this because he had killed an old grand army man over the price of a glass of beer. The mob was looking for another dago who had helped him dispose of the body. I was anxious to get home as soon as possible, so I rode the fifty-five trifles into town in the early afternoon and found everything in an uproar. There were thousands of excited people parading up and down the streets and even out into the country. Some of them appeared to be looking for someone to beat up on, and I began to think it might be anyone, so I felt pretty humble as I peddled my way through the streets on my way home.

As the jail was not far out of my way, I thought I would ride by there and see what damage had been done. I did not think they would be looking for the other dago in that location, at least not riding a bicycle. Well, there was a great hole in the brick wall that the mob had made to get the prisoner out, and the tree where they had hanged the dago was just a hole in the ground. They had literally torn it to pieces and dug out the roots, I suppose for keepsakes, to remind them of the pleasant evening they had spent there at the necktie party.

I went on home, and the folks told me how the old grand army man had gone into a dago saloon for a glass of beer, and when he had drank the beer, he found out that he did not have the cents to pay for it. One dago killed him and the other dragged the body out in the backyard, but it seems they were caught and put in jail. Then the mob took the murderer out, and I have already told what they did to him. They were now looking for his accomplice, but it seemed the authorities had hidden him away somewhere.

That night, I thought I would go downtown and see what was going on, leaving my wheel at home, as I feared someone might want it to ride to Washington, DC. Coxey's Army was taking all means of conveyances they could get possession of, even capturing freight trains, engines and all, and loading them up with, not hoboes, but just men who had no jobs. Some of them were hungry, and some had families who were lacking the necessities of life right there in the midst of plenty; they had no money to buy what they needed.

I have often wondered at the fierceness of a mob, but I was to learn something more about it within the next few weeks and even this very evening. As I came into the main streets of the city, I soon found myself right in the center of a milling, noisy mob of people looking for the other man to hang. And you may say you would not join a mob in taking a person's life, but I found that when I got in there, it was hard to get out without getting knocked down and trampled underfoot. So for a while, I became part of the mob, as the crowd surged back and forth, attracted this way or that by any sudden commotion. Then someone shouted, "Here he is!" and with one impulse, I could feel myself being pushed along, and there was no use in resisting. Well, it proved to be another false alarm, as there had been many, and finally, as the crowd commenced to thin out a little, I gradually worked my way out and went home without seeing a man hanged. To this day, I am not sorry, for the man finally had a fair trial and was sentenced to twenty years in prison. This didn't end the excitement though, for, as is always the case in times like these, when the political pot got to boiling over.

I never was much of a politician, and of course, at that time, I was almost too young to bother my head with politics. As near as I can remember, with Dad's help (Dad was a real Democrat), there had been a city election, and the old police board had refused, for some reason or other, to vacate city hall and make room for the new board. They called out the state troops, wheeled out a few Gatling guns and cannons, and trained them on the front of the city hall, ordering them to get out or else. But then, nothing else happened, and the old officials just came to the front and made fun of the state militia by waving their arms this way and that in mockery, helping them to sight the field guns.

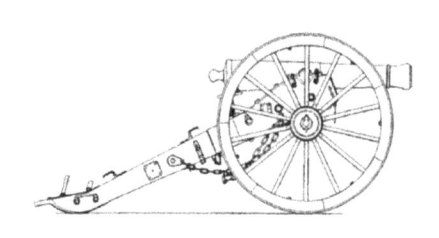

Well, it was lots of fun for the crowd, and every building was lined with people, wherever they could get a place where they could sit or stand or hang on—in the windows, doors, or on the roof—and the streets were blocked with humanity hungry to see the fun. I suppose if one of those cannons had boomed out and started the real thing, there would have been a real scramble to get out of there, and many would have been hurt or killed. But the bluff did not work, although the state troops camped on the street for a while until the governor of the state (Governor Waite) got permission to call the government troops from Fort Logan. Then things began to happen.

I was at the depot when they landed there, and when they marched up Seventeenth Street, looking so efficient and businesslike, the would-be hecklers fell back and gave them room, and no questions were asked. A feeling of pride came over me then, as I witnessed the businesslike efficiency of Uncle Sam's army. Well, they were only a very small sample of the real thing, which has three times since then caused the world to sit up and take notice. What they were then and in my father's time, they still are, and I pray to God always will be until the time comes when there shall be no need of them anymore. "When the knowledge of God shall cover the earth as the waters cover the sea, and the soldiers of the battlefield will be supplemented by the soldiers of the Cross, and they shall beat their swords into plowshares and their spears into pruning hooks, and they shall not learn war anymore." (Isaiah 2:4)

To those who may cast their eyes over this manuscript, I will say that it may stand out plainly that I believe in a God who will someday rule this world in peace and righteousness. And that when such times as I have been telling about will be a thing of the past. When people shall have learned the lesson that they cannot run this world without God, the Creator of it. Needless to say, the city hall row was soon settled, and the very fact that Uncle Sam's boys were there was all that was necessary, and there was not a shot fired.

One night, I saw a big light downtown and got on my wheel and got down there just in time to see a new six-story building burn to the ground. The Union Depot was also badly damaged by fire around the same time. Coxey's army was strung all across the nation trying to get to Washington, as they wanted to force congress to do something to relieve the distressing situation, but as I remember it, they might as well have stayed at home.

As I have mentioned before, I was trying to find something to do to help out a little, and during that year, I got a few days' work here and there at a variety of different jobs. These jobs ranged from digging ditches and laying sewer pipe to digging spuds at a dollar a day plus board. Another fellow and I got a job on the section near Trinidad, Colorado, for a dollar and forty cents a day, and paid four dollars and fifty cents a week for board. We worked about a month and a half and got fired because I got mad at the boss and told him something I will not repeat here. We had earned enough money to pay our fare back to Denver, but we had made up our minds that we were not going to give it back to the railroad company.

We beat our way back on two freight trains, covering about 216 miles. It was late in November and freezing cold weather, and our first ride was in an open stock car loaded with coal. The wind was howling through the open cracks, and we nearly froze before we got to Pueblo, which was somewhere near halfway.

Well, that was the first time I ever beat my way, but my partner was an old hand at the game. He was a very homely man. When he started to cry because the brakeman was going to put us off, the look on my partner's face, along with the fifty cents I gave the brakeman, paid our fare over that division. We got into Pueblo about midnight and went to a cheap hotel and got a bed and slept until late, then got our breakfast and a couple of sandwiches to stick in our pockets. Then we went out to the railroad yards and saw a freight train standing on the track with a caboose on the south end of it. There was nothing on the other end, so we asked the switchman where the train was going. He said to Denver and that it would be leaving soon, so we mooched around until we found an end door that was loose and crawled in and closed the door.

We found that we still had a carload of coal under us to bed down on, but this time we had a boxcar around us to break the wind. Well, we did not have to wait long until we were awakened by a terrific jolt, ending our dreams of better things to come. We were moved several feet in the direction we did not wish to go, but after a series of bangs and crashes and the squeaking of brakes, we were on our way on the long cold ride to Denver. I said I had never stolen anything after I had my "shooting-star" experience, but I guess this was a justified steal, as we had worked for this railroad company for a month and a half for almost nothing. Besides, if we would have paid our fare, we would have arrived home just about broke. The brakeman never even knew we were on the train. So it was a complete steal, as far as stealing a ride was concerned.

Our next concern was to find out when we were approaching Denver so that we could leave the train before we got into the freight yards, as there was danger of being taken in for vagrancy. We managed to peek out occasionally through a crack in the door, and when we saw the lights of the city (for it was late at night), we crawled out on the bumpers. When the train slowed down for a crossing, we jumped off and walked several miles into town. If we were not bums, we must have looked it after riding all that distance on a carload of coal. When I got home, I came in the back way surprising the folks of course, by my sudden appearing and by the way I must have looked. Well, we built up a fire, and I took a bath and threw my old clothes into the backyard and got a clean outfit. If there was any livestock [*bedbugs*] left over after I had sold my bed at the section house to another bum, I never took any of them home to Mother. And so ended my one and only railroad experience as a section hand.

As there was nothing to do around town, I started a little shop in Dad's coal shed. Through the balance of that winter, I done a variety of jobs, such as repairing furniture, making picture frames and inlaid woodwork, which was a kind of a hobby of mine. If I couldn't sell the work outright, I would either raffle it off or give it away to some girl I was a little smitten on. There was one who lived next door whom I made the Indian clubs for. They were inlaid in stripes, like a striped sock, and when I went to see her swing them at a church entertainment, she nearly fainted when she saw me in the audience. I do not know why, but maybe it was because of her surprise at seeing me in church. She was a very pretty girl, and if I had not been so bashful, I might have been able to drive away some of the monotony by having a good time with her, but I was modest, and so was she. About the only pleasure I ever got out of our little affair was to admire her at a safe distance. When her family gave a farewell party for me at their house the night before I left for Wyoming, they sang that old familiar goodbye song, "God Be With You Till We Meet Again." I had tears in my eyes, and she looked sad about something, and that was the parting of the ways for us, as I never saw her again.

While working in the little shop, I made several center tables. I finished one that I had started while working in the mill which is in our home today. It has around four or five thousand pieces of different shapes and several kinds of wood in it and, after fifty-two years, is still in a good state of preservation.

One job that I took on that winter I will mention because it figures in with things that are yet to happen out in the Wyoming hills. A fellow had an old guitar that had been so badly wrecked that it was completely out of commission. He brought the pieces to me, asking if I would fix it up for him, as it had been a very fine-sounding instrument. Well, that was out of my line, but I told him I would take it. I went to work on it and succeeded to the extent that he was pretty well-pleased with it. Then when he went to play the chords on it, I took in the harmony and tried to get the fingering positions to the major chords in my mind so that I would remember them. Then he gave me five dollars and went away satisfied. The man did not know that I had taken all the measurements, as well as having placed the guitar on a piece of heavy paper and traced the shape of it. This way, I could have it all for future reference, and so I put the plans and figures away in my toolbox. That is the way his old wreck of a guitar became the model of the first guitar I ever made, and what I had committed to memory from his playing became my first and only lesson in playing and tuning the guitar. Later, this would help me beat the loneliness out there in the hills of Wyoming.

Ranching and Tragedy in Wyoming

As springtime came around again and there seemed little prospect of the labor situation getting any better, I commenced to think of the ranch again. I realized that if I were out there, I could help the boys and at least earn my board.

I turned my wheel back to the party I had bought it from, still owing some money on it. Then one morning, I think it was in April, I meandered my way out to the railroad yards. I climbed onto a flat car loaded with big slabs of granite, which was even harder than coal, and rode the car to near Greely, Colorado. There I fell in with another fellow who was going my way, and as I had no prior right over that section of the railroad and he did not object to my company, we hoboed it along together for part of the journey.

When we got to Cheyenne, the cops got hold of us and took us to police headquarters, where they made us show that we had a few dollars and then let us go. That was the nearest I ever came to sleeping in jail. They told us to get out of town, which we proceeded to do, walking the track against a terrible cold west wind on the steep climb toward Sherman Hill. It was after nightfall, and the cold wind cut through our thin clothes like a knife. We finally came to a water tank that was partly enclosed underneath and went inside. It was floored with ice, with a couple of square timbers partially embedded in the ice, and big drops of cold water leaking down from the tank. We bedded down on the timbers and tried to sleep, but every time we fell asleep, we found ourselves rolling off our perch onto the ice and water. This was how we spent the night, and as soon as it was daylight, we pulled out on the long hard hike toward the top of the Rockies, where I had celebrated my former bicycle climb by taking a header.

Well, we puffed along up the hill against the wind for several miles, and then we stopped and looked back toward Cheyenne and saw a freight train puffing along. It seemed to be having about as hard a time as we were. We reasoned that 350 pounds would not make that much difference to it and would make a lot of difference to us. We planned how we were to board it as it came along, my partner taking one end of a certain car and me taking the other. It is needless to say that they did not stop for us, so we had to catch her on the fly. The brakeman proved to be human, so he opened up the end door to a boxcar at the first stop and let us inside. I gave him my jackknife, and he let me ride to my destination, while the other fellow they took up on the engine to shovel coal.

At Laramie, another bunch got on our car, and some of them were pretty tough-looking. I kept my eyes open, fearing that they might swipe my meal ticket. When the train was pulling into Rock Creek, I wanted to be sure of getting off as the train might not stop. When it slowed down a little, I jumped off and rolled over several times before I found the bottom of the grade. Then the train slowed down and stopped. What a world! I got scratched up a little but was able to take on a good feed when I got to the boarding house, and that was the last time I ever beat my way on a train.

I caught a ride out to the ranch the next day with some friends who were in for supplies. I found the boys well and making preparations for planting, but before I go on with this part of my story, I think I shall go back and tell of an experience I had during the first year I was in Wyoming in 1892.

There was a man in our community who was a dealer in horses, and he would buy up a bunch of horses of all kinds, mostly bad outlaws and wild broncs, and drive them back to Kansas or Nebraska. He would sell them to the farmers or trade them off, anything to make money out of them. His idea was to hitch up a different horse to the wagon every time he made camp, and in that way he managed to have them partly broke by the time he got down there, therefore, to get a better price for them.

Well, he offered me twenty dollars a month and my fare back if I would go with him on a trip, and although I had been warned that he was an awful crank, I thought it would give me a good chance to earn a few dollars and maybe see old Kansas again. Now I had never had any experience in handling wild broncos, but nevertheless took the job, thinking that I might learn something about it, which I did in a very hard way. I had helped break a few Kansas horses, but I might as well say right here that as a rule an unbroken Wyoming bronc is ten times worse than an unbroken farm horse. We were to change off in the work, each driving the team half a day or so, and then riding the horse and driving the herd of broncs the other half.

My first lesson was learning how to get onto a horse and stay there. But the first time, I didn't stay, as I tried to get on the horse like we did down on the farm in Kansas. Instead of landing in the saddle, I landed behind the horse on the ground. Of course, the boss had a good laugh, but I failed to see or feel anything to laugh about. Then he showed me how to do it, with the result that when the horse made a lunge, I landed in the saddle and stayed there. I think we made about forty miles the first day, and there was no change of jobs. I rode the horse and drove the herd all day, and I was never so sore in my life. I wished I was back on Cow Creek, but the *Old Book* says, "He that turns back is not worthy of me," and then I had a good bump of determination in my head, and there was no turning back.

He let me drive the team the next forenoon, and this was not much of a relief, as the wagon seat was just a board. The roadway, part of the way, was down an old rocky creek bed, and it was about as hard to keep my seat as it had been on the horse's back. That noon, we caught up a green horse and hitched him to the wagon, along with one that was supposed to be broken. We caught an old gentle-looking pony with saddle marks on his back, thinking perhaps it would make things a little easier for me after my hard ride the day before.

We saddled him up and tied the bridle reins to a fencepost so I could help Mr. "M" with the team, but when I went to look for my horse, he was gone. I spotted him up on the side of a hill known as Iron Mountain, and he stood very nicely for me to catch him, but when I tried to get on, he threw down his head and made a big lunge. I landed about six feet down the mountainside, with my knee striking a sharp rock, and as it was my left knee I could not bend it to get my foot in the stirrup for mounting my horse. Well, Mr. "M" had to do the riding for a while until I could use my leg again but only for a day or so. It proved later that the old saddle-marked pony was an old outlaw, and only an expert could ride him. I never tried him again.

Nothing much out of the usual line of events took place until we got as far as Sterling, Colorado. At about that time, things began to happen that finally caused me to tell him to get someone else to take my place and I would quit. It is sufficient to say that he proved to be just what they said he was, an old crank. He had traded for three horses at Sterling. One was a horse that would strike with her front feet when I tried to get on her and throw herself over backward when I tried to ride her. She was a very treacherous beast, but I finally rode her, as I had learned a few things about bad horses on the trip. This knowledge came in handy when later I started in the stock business for myself. Another one he traded for was a little blue Indian pony that had seen better days but still knew how to buck long and hard, as I will tell about later. Mr. "M" soon found a man to take my place, and we settled our account by him giving me old Blue Dog even up for my service.

There I was, 240 miles from home, with only two or three dollars in my pocket to get home on and a very slow old pony to ride. Of course, I had my saddle and saddle blanket, along with forty feet of saddle rope I could use to tie my horse out with at night and at noon to let him rest for a while.

As I looked off into the west across the rolling plains, I thought of Kansas, but there was no sign of human habitation for miles. Just here and there, an old deserted homestead shack that had long since fallen into ruins, relics of the blighted hopes of pioneers who had tried and failed. But here it was worse as water in places could be as far as twenty miles or more away. This was the one and only time since I had left Kansas that I was out of sight of the mountains.

Before I tell of my trip back over the desert, I will tell of what happened on the south side of the river, just before Mr. "M" and I parted company. The South Platte River at Sterling was a series of small channels running between sandbars and islands covered with willows or some kind of small growth. It was spanned by a long narrow bridge. We crossed the bridge and made camp at a bend in the river where we thought it would be a good place to hold the horses overnight. All went well until about sundown, but then the mosquitoes came in clouds and settled down on the horses, driving them out into the sand hills about two miles or so. We did not get them back until nearly noon the next day. Mr. "M" wanted me to help him get started on his way, so I saddled up the mare that he and I had traded for, and then she reared up and fell back with me twice before I could persuade her to keep her front feet on the ground. Each time, I barely got out of her way before she hit the ground, and if she had caught me, this story would never have been told. Well, she was reasonably gentle after we got on the way, and I had no further trouble with her.

We found that the land east and south of the river was very nice and level once we got out beyond the sand hills, which extended out from the river for some distance. There was some dry farming going on there even at that time in 1892. There were some very nice fields of small grain, which seemed to be just in the critical stage of maturing into crops, but they were badly in need of a good rain. From my Kansas experiences, I could tell about how much dry weather a crop could stand, and it appeared just a few more days of hot, dry weather would end the prospects of a crop for another year. I had noticed a heavy rain cloud forming in the northwest and thought about what a godsend it could be to those farmers. As I speculated about whether it would hit us or go around to the north, it commenced to break up and go around.

About that time, we were driving the horses between two fields of grain and were having a hard time keeping them out of it, when I saw a man without a hat riding a powerful black horse. He was riding bareback with a work bridle. The man too was a powerful big fellow, and he was coming toward us at full speed. I could tell he was mad, and I was a little scared for a spell, but when he commenced to shake his fist at the cloud and swear, I knew it was not us he was mad at and felt relieved. He had ridden out to help us get through with the horses, so they would not tramp on the grain. He was a foreigner, a Dane I think, but he knew how to use the English language when it came to swearing, even cursing God himself.

They were magnificent specimens of humanity and horseflesh. The man, I suppose, would weigh well over two hundred pounds, and the horse, seventeen hundred, at least. I thought if I had been the owner of our bunch, I would have gladly traded the whole outfit with the wagon thrown in for this one horse, and I believe I would have made a good deal. As for the man, I have often thought of how his energy was worse than wasted in cursing his Creator. Since becoming a Christian, I know how much better it would have been for him to have gone to some quiet place and prayed to his Creator to forgive his sins and then placed the rain question in God's hands. I think this section of country I have been telling about, years later, became part of the *Great Dust Bowl*. If that man was a fair representation of that community, I do not wonder that God withheld the rain until they learned some sense.

Well, this incident ended my trip east, and I caught old Blue Dog, put my saddle on him and started back. It was nearly sundown when I got back to Sterling. I found a place where there was a pretty good pasture and picketed my horse out, went into town and bought some things for lunch, and then went back to old Blue dog to settle down and eat. Then, with my saddle for a pillow and one fold of my saddle blanket over me, the other under me, I spent the night trying to sleep. Although it was the first of July, the nights were pretty cold so I slept very little. As soon as it was light, after eating some cheese and crackers, we got a drink and then started our day's journey which followed along the railroad for some distance.

We had made about twenty miles by noon and found an artesian well there. Old Blue dog and I filled up our tanks, but when I went to look at my grub pack, the sack had broken open and all I had left was two cans of salmon. We drank some more water and continued our journey and then I began to get sick. By the time I got to a place where there was an old deserted shack, I was so sick that I just had to stop for the night. The wind was blowing something fierce and the old house rattled and groaned and squeaked. I found some old rags and sacks and put my blanket over me and tried to sleep, but it was like a nightmare. It sounded like all the devils in Hades had been turned loose, and my physical condition did not help things very much. Well, I did not want any more salmon after that for a long time.

As I had eaten neither supper nor breakfast, by the next day I was feeling pretty weak. That day, we came to a little place where there was a store, so I went in and bought a few things I thought I could eat. I got a little coffee and some sugar and picked up an old can, and when I got to a place where there was some water, I washed up the can and myself a little. Then I gathered some trash together and made a fire and soon I had some good hot coffee. By the time I had finished my meal, I felt like a new man. That night, we were getting back to where people lived again, and after giving

Old Blue a drink and a good place to eat, I burrowed down in a haystack and had a real good night's sleep.

The next day I made it to Cheyenne. I have forgotten to mention that like all other would-be cowboys, on my way down, I had bought myself a ten-gallon hat, as they call them these days. My financial means were limited, but I got all the hat I could with the money I had, and that was plenty. We had gone through a rainy period, and the rain had taken all the starch out of the hat, and it now had the habit of flopping down around my face and neck. I must have been a tough-looking guy, and it did not help matters any that my clothes were dirty and I had not shaved for some time.

When I presented myself to the citizens of Cheyenne on this July the fourth (although I did not know it was the fourth), I must have been a worse-looking spectacle than I would be nearly two years later when I was taken to police headquarters [mentioned earlier], but those old cow towns will excuse a lot more in this kind of makeup (like a guy on a horse) than they will in a common boxcar hobo.

Old Blue and I paraded down the street and came to a roped-off place where they were putting on all kinds of stunts. There were foot races, high jumps, and everything else that goes into the making of a Fourth of July celebration, except the bronco busting. This part of the program, and unknown to me, I was to furnish. For just as I reached the intersection where they were doing the stunts, Old Blue decided it was about time to perform and started in. Of all the bucking he ever did while I owned him, he gave his best exhibition right there on the streets of Cheyenne, just where it would do the most good to everybody but me.

With the old hat flopping down over my head and my untidy appearance, I must have been a great attraction. The crowd forgot everything else and gave me their whole attention judging by their yelling and guying. I guess I was the only one who was not enjoying it. When Blue dog finally quit, he had both me and the saddle right up on top of his shoulders, ready to pitch us off in the street. I got off and straightened up my saddle and went on my way, and as far as Old Blue was concerned, the Fourth of July was over. I put him away and went back and saw the rest of the show, but no one offered to pass the hat for me.

That night, I went to a hotel, cleaned up as best I could, and had my supper. Then I went to bed and had a good night's sleep on what little money I had left. That is, it took just about all I had, and by the time I paid for my breakfast and bought some bread and cold meat and things for my lunches along the way, I don't think I had a quarter left. I want to say right here that in all my experiences, I have never asked for anything to eat that I did not have the money to pay for. If I did not have the money, I went without. I guess it was my pride mixed in with plenty of bashfulness that caused some of my independence. I suppose some would call it an inferiority complex these days.

The next morning, I pulled out for the north along the route we had taken on our way down. We went through the gates of old Fort D.A. Russell, and Uncle Sam did not object to our going through. The Cheyenne Northern ran almost parallel with the wagon road at least part of the way. We stopped for the night not far from the railroad tracks, where there were some pieces of old railroad ties, and I made up a good fire with the free wood. I was fairly comfortable on one side at a time as long as I kept the fire burning. It was a very beautiful moonlit night, and the coyotes were making melodies on all sides. I do not know whether they were waiting for Old Blue to kick off, or me, but I know we foiled that, at least for the time (they may have got Old Blue later).

Fort D. A. Russell in Wyoming, circa 1900

As I sat there that night, with no sign of humanity within miles, a terrible feeling of loneliness came over me and I longed for some human being to talk to. When I finally lay down and seemingly had gone to sleep, I thought I heard my brother Aaron calling me, saying, "Come over here." I asked, "Where?" and he said, "Over here, in this pit." When I awoke, I was standing and looking down into a deep ditch that the railroad company had made when putting in the fill. I began to wonder just how much longer it would be good for me to be alone, as I had heard that sometimes being alone too long affects people's minds. Then I was more anxious to get back to the ranch than ever, but Old Blue was only good for about forty miles a day at best, and I still had about eighty miles to go. That meant one more night alone on the range. Well, it may be all right to sing about, but the reality is not so good, at least not for some people. I was to become more reconciled to being alone later on, but not out on the open range where the coyotes howl on all sides.

The next day by noon, we were at the foot of Iron Mountain, where the outlaw horse had thrown me off. There was an electrical storm going on at the top of the mountain, and as it was a mountain of solid iron ore (so they said), it attracted the lightning. As I traveled on over the top of the range, I looked back once in a while and could see the cloud covering the mountaintop. When I stopped for the night at a bridge that crossed the Big Laramie River, I could still watch the lightning flashing around the top of the mountain, while there was no other place on the whole horizon where there was a cloud. Well, you will say this was a small thing to write about, but it furnished a very lonely boy with part of an evening's entertainment, and I was glad for it.

That night, I slept (or tried to sleep) under a small bridge that covered a dry slough close to the main bridge that crossed the Big Laramie River. It was about five miles from the famous McGill ranch where I could have found plenty to eat, a good bed, feed for my horse, and last but not least, human companionship. What was true of the McGill ranch was true of all ranches in that part of Wyoming at that time, the bill was already paid. The place where I slept is now covered with water, for it became the site of a great reservoir.

The next day, I arrived back at the ranch in time to help the boys with the hay harvest, and we were fairly busy through the rest of the season. As far as we were concerned, we were pretty well contented until I got the notion to go back to Denver the next spring. I have already told of that winter's work of hauling the hay to Rock Creek and the damage of the year or so that followed, and now I must take up my story again where I came back to the ranch in the spring of 1894.

I do not recall in detail the things that happened that summer, only that I helped the boys with the irrigating and putting up the hay. But I recall one thing very distinctly that took place when we were baling hay. We had rented an old hay baler that was what was called a half-circle press. That is, the team would go around in a half circle and the plunger would fly back, and then the driver would swing the team around, and they would pull back the other way. It required a person to drive the team all the time the thing was in motion. We were in the habit of changing off at the work so that it would not be too hard on any one of us. I was the one driving on the day the accident happened.

Elmer was pitching from the stack, and Aaron was feeding the press when I heard Aaron yell. Before I could stop the team, his foot was caught in the press in such a way that it was badly crushed. Well, we got him to the house, but we had nothing to put on it to ease the pain. We did not know what to do, so I saddled up one of the horses and rode eight miles to a ranch where I thought they might have something to help. The lady gave me some dope that she thought would help and told me to apply hot cloths to Aaron's foot and to keep them hot by wringing them out with hot water. When I got back after riding the sixteen miles, his foot was all swollen up and as black as it could be. I at once got busy with the hot cloths and kept it up for a long time and then applied the dope. That kind of treatment was all it ever got, and within a few days, he was tying bales by placing his knee on a chair and using it as a crutch to walk around on. We were pretty badly scared for a while but glad that it was no worse, of course.

Well, times were not so prosperous on the ranch, but we had the advantage over the city dweller. We were able to raise plenty of such kinds of vegetables that would grow at that elevation, like potatoes, rutabagas, cabbage, onions, and so forth. The meat question was settled by our going out on the plains and killing a half-dozen antelope, hanging them up, and letting them freeze up for the winter. There was elk and deer in the hills and plenty of grouse. While the city people were finding it hard to live in some cases, we had plenty to eat, and about all it cost, besides flour, sugar, coffee, lard, and some dried fruit, was just a little healthy exercise. Just such conditions as these were what caused me to be back in the hills again. Not so much from choice, perhaps, as from necessity.

I remember one fall when all three of us went up the creek with the team, about five or six miles, and were hauling building timber out of the hills. After we had gotten out a load of logs, Elmer and I decided to let Aaron take the load home while we took another route home over a high ridge. On our way back, he carried the rifle, and I, the shotgun. When we had gone some distance, we decided to separate, he going down one side of the ridge and me the other. We had only gone a short distance when I heard a shot from the direction in which he had gone. As there was only one shot and Elmer was rather inexperienced with a rifle at that time, I hurried over there, thinking he might have had an accident. Just as I entered a little grove, there stood Elmer beside the biggest pair of elk horns I think I ever saw, and attached to the horns was a big bull elk as large as a three-year-old steer.

Whether he was more pleased or surprised, I was not quite able to figure out, as this was his first elk and he was very young at the time. I asked him where he had hit him, and he said, "I guess I must have scared him to death because I can't find the bullet hole." He bled him with his jackknife, the same way we would have bled a beef, and we found that the bullet had broken the elk's neck. So there we were, with that huge animal and nothing to take him apart with but our pocketknife. We were about six miles from home, and it was getting late in the afternoon, so we went to work and succeeded in skinning, dressing, and quartering him. Then we took off the head and hung the quarters up in the trees, all before nightfall. We got back to the ranch long after dark, and if Aaron had been worried about us, he never said a thing about it that I can remember.

The next day, we went back with the team and got as close as we could with the wagon. We took old Patch (Jack wouldn't work at this kind of a job), and by cutting a trail part of the way, we succeeded in packing the meat and hide out. By the time we got home it was nearly nightfall. There was an old bachelor I'll call Cliff, who lived about two miles from us, and he was a good antelope hunter. When he got an antelope, he would almost always bring us a hindquarter. So when he came along later, we told him we would like to give him a hindquarter of the elk. When he looked at the hindquarter, he said, "Yes, old Two Bar." That was the brand of the cattle that ranged that part of the country at the time. People were always kidding each other about eating "Two Bar beef" whether they were guilty or not, and Cliff would not believe it was an elk until we showed him the hide.

Well, as the long, cold snowy winter closed in around us, it seemed best to try to find something to do. Elmer had got possession of a violin somehow, and he sat around a good part of the time scraping on that fiddle. It used to be pretty hard to take, but finally, we could occasionally hear some sort of noise that sounded a little like the starting of a tune. Before long, I began to think of the plans and specifications I had stored away in my tool chest for the guitar I might make some day, and I decided to make out an order to Montgomery Ward and Company for the parts I needed. I thought it might be a good way to get even with Elmer for all of those unearthly noises he was making. So I made out an order for some strings, frets, and keys. From some wood I had stored away, along with some cedar from the nearby hills, I started to build a guitar. By the time my other fixtures arrived, I had it pretty well underway.

Local homesteaders and musicians from the Garrett, Wyoming community. Robert is the man standing in the back holding his handmade guitar. Photo circa 1902

It was with a great deal of anticipation that I put the strings in place and commenced to wind them up. When I finally had two or more strings tuned so they would harmonize, I thought it was the sweetest music I had ever heard, and before long I could play some of the chords. Although neither Elmer nor I ever had a music lesson in our lives, the loneliness of the hills, it seems, forced us to do something like this. It was only for our own amusement at first, but soon we were playing at the old-time dances, thus providing the only public amusement available in that place and time. I hardly ever play anymore, but the guitar is still my favorite instrument.

There is something else I would like to say while I have mentioned the subject of these old-time dances. If the members of so-called modern civilization were as respectful in their conduct toward the opposite sex as people were back then, and if they would cut out the booze and cigarettes, we would have a better world to live in. We would also have a better chance of obtaining a home in heaven, even though it takes something more than how we pursue amusement to get one ready for that home over there. I shall say more about this later on if God is willing to let me live that long.

About this time, Aaron became interested in prospecting and mining and started being away most of the time. And since Elmer was planning to file on a piece of land and build a home of his own, it was clear someone else would soon get possession of the ranch. I was alone quite a bit, and I would get so lonely, I could hardly stand it there at times. Sometimes I would pull out, hike several miles to a neighbor's place, and stay a while. Then I would hike back and feel better for a while, but soon the old lonely feeling would come back again, and even the old guitar could not cheer me up.

How I got through those lonely, cold, and cheerless winters is still a mystery to me, as there was nothing much to do. I eventually got busy on another guitar, made almost entirely out of native wood, and this occupied my time for a while. I would play one for a while and then the other and speculate on which was the best-toned. Then I made one of oak, all except the face of it, and hand-carved the back of it, which took a lot of time. Then later, I started to make one that would be inlaid all over with some thousand pieces of wood, but I was a long time getting it finished. In fact, I was not to complete it until later, when I had a place of my own to work in.

That spring, the old place was sold, and I got the old team and wagon for what I had put into it. Aaron said I could have the old cabin on the creek below, and as it was not in the place where I wanted it, I tore it down and put it in a more sheltered spot. Then I got out some logs and built a small barn. Although I had never filed on the land, I knew the squatter's right would hold the claim or give me the first right, according to law. Therefore, I was in no hurry about filing, as I needed all the money I could get to fix the thing up. Well, I dug ditches, cleared land, and planted spuds. Then I sold the spuds wherever I could get a market, sometimes hauling them as far as thirty-five miles to the railroad, but mostly selling them to the ranchers who did not care to bother with raising their own. I also dug a potato cellar large enough to hold over twenty tons, and I was pretty well-contented now that I had something to do.

Although it was a lonely life, I found out that the best cure for loneliness was to interest oneself in something worthwhile and work on the job as much as possible. There was great satisfaction in knowing that there was no one else who had a stake in what I was doing. Although it was a humble beginning, my personal requirements at that time were small, and I remained pretty independent for a while. I was satisfied just to live a simple life, not bothering my head too much about getting anything ahead. This was the state of affairs for a while. Then things began to happen that would change my whole perspective on life.

It would be a strange story indeed, if there were no romance connected with it. And I would be an abnormal human being if I did not respond to those romantic impulses that God has put within every normal human being. Well, I had had several mild cases thus far in my life, but the real thing had not yet jarred my rather peaceable and contented nature so far. I was no exception to the rule however, and this is the way it happened for me. We got our mail at a ranch about twelve miles away where they kept the post office. It was our custom, when we went to the post office, to bring the mail for all the ranchers along the road, each one taking his turn. In that way, we were spared many unnecessary trips. As my place was almost the farthest away from the office, and as the people who kept the office were friends of mine, I would often stay all night and help the family with their chores. This little bit of work around the place gave me a way to pay for my meals, bed, and horse feed, and was also a chance for a visit with the neighbors.

As I have mentioned, it was customary in Wyoming at that time for anyone who happened around at mealtime to stop and eat, and sometimes sleep, as it was often very far between ranches. Anyone so benefitting would most likely have the chance to return the favor very soon. If there was no one at home, a person was supposed to go in, make himself something to eat, and stay the night if necessary. You just had to wash the dishes and leave the house in as good a condition as it was when you came.

Well anyway, as I rode up to the house this particular evening to leave the outgoing mail, I noticed a horse tied to the hitching pole with a blanket and a surcingle but no saddle. I wondered who would ride a horse like that in this part of the world. When I entered the house, I was introduced to a young lady who was the neighborhood schoolteacher, and I found her to be one of the friendliest females I had ever met. Somehow, she seemed different from any girl I had ever known before, and after we had a little talk together, she mounted her horse and rode away. I could not forget her, and I longed to follow after her and get better acquainted, but my better judgment said no.

I tried to content myself with just the remembrance of her, but after several days of this trying to live on a memory, I got up the courage to go and see her. I asked her to go to a dance with me, and of course, she did not turn me down. I asked how she would prefer to go, with a rig or on horseback, and she asked me to bring an extra horse but no saddle. That was the way she rode, with just a heavy blanket that was made for that purpose, and she could surely ride, for she had been raised on a cow ranch and knew all there was to know about a ranch.

She was the only child of a widow who had a cattle ranch about sixty-five miles from my hangout. I will call her "Miss D," as her earthly vision will never look upon the pages of this manuscript, for she has gone to a better world now. There is no longer the least spark of bitterness in my heart toward her for the way she treated me, nor do I blame her for turning me down. At the time of our association, I had nothing to keep a wife on and was making no special effort to acquire such means, so I have her to thank for one thing. She stirred me up to the determination to show the world I could succeed.

Our association extended over a period of nearly three years, and I will not try to make a love story out of this, for there were times when we were not in perfect harmony. Therefore, I am sure as far as we both were concerned that it was better that it ended as it did. She was inclined to want to have other fellows on her string, and of course, that kept me guessing as to just where I was on the string. So the last time I went to see her, I told her it would be the last time I would come, but I guess she thought I did not mean it.

I kept my word, and the only time I ever saw her again was at a dance. I danced with her, and for that brief time, we both seemed to be reliving the good times we had shared, and after a brief talk with her, we parted. She soon married the other fellow and so ended the first real romance of my life. I was to have about three more, but there was to be something more substantial about them, at least the last two, for it was not long before I was engaged to another. It soon was broken up, and I was free and so was she, and she married before I did.

About this time, there was a neighbor who wanted to buy me out, and I sold out to him pretty cheap. I put the money in the bank and went to work on a ranch for thirty-five dollars a month and board. I worked for this man, Mr. Atkinson, about two years, during which time I saved my money, and in the meantime I filed on a homestead near the place I had just sold. Between work time, I built a cabin, according to law, and there was some meadow on the place.

So then I bought three cows with calves and seven head of yearling heifers. And then I let Mr. "C", who had bought my squatter's right, run them for me with his cattle with the understanding that he could have the hay and range on my place. In that way, I soon had a herd of cattle started.

I went on with the work I was doing, helping Mr. Atkinson build up his ranch. It was out on the Red Desert, as I called it, for there was not a tree on the place. But there was a stream of water running through it which came from a large, always-open spring about a mile above his land. We had a lot of ditching to do as well as building and fencing. We had to go back in the hills ten to fifteen miles to get out the timber and fence posts, and there was always lots of hard work to do. We would start early in the morning with two teams, and sometimes it would be after dark before we got back with our loads. It was the kind of work that builds up a good, rugged constitution, which does not hurt a person, as long as it is not overdone.

Felix Atkinson Ranch on Sheep Creek (Laramie Republican, December 1, 1901)

Lizzy and Felix Atkinson. (Photo taken in Laramie, Wyoming, in 1896, courtesy of Catherine Atkinson.)

As soon as we had the house ready to live in, Mrs. Atkinson was in need of help. She was on the way to having her second baby, and for a time, Mr. Atkinson had hired another man to help with ditching, which made extra work for her. They hired a young girl from a new family that had just moved in about twelve miles above Mr. Atkinson's ranch to help with the work. I will never forget my first introduction to Miss Dollie Cameron.

One day, the other hired man and I took one of the team and went into the hills to get some poles for fencing or roofing purposes. When we had the first load of poles cut and loaded up, the other fellow took the load to the ranch, and I stayed to cut the next load. Well, I had only cut a few poles when my axe glanced and cut my foot so bad that I could hardly walk. I was wearing high-top boots, so I sat down and pulled off my boot. It was bleeding pretty badly, so I wrapped it up in a red bandana handkerchief, which was the only thing I had that I could use for this purpose. I pulled my boot back on and went on with cutting my load. When Mr. Atkinson got back, I had the load ready for him, but by the time we got back to the ranch, we had to cut the boot from top to bottom to get it off. Miss Cameron was there, and she seemed so sympathetic as she watched Mrs. Atkinson fix up my crippled foot, that it rather appealed to me. Well, I still have the scar as a reminder of the happenings of that day.

The next day was Sunday, and I took advantage of this opportunity to get acquainted with the young lady. Of course, when two young people of the opposite sex are thrown together under those kind of circumstances, they are most likely to become either attracted to each other or just the opposite. It has been my experience that it is pretty hard to be indifferent under such conditions. When one day, another fellow got fresh with her, I bawled him out. I guess that helped my case along a little, for she did not like fresh guys any better than I did. As time went by and we spent most of our spare time together, our mutual understanding got to the place where we were soon engaged to be married.

As she was not yet eighteen and I had no place to keep a wife, we decided to wait until I could build a house on my homestead and get things in better condition financially. I continued working for Mr. Atkinson, and she wanted to work too, so for a while, she had a job in a home about sixty or seventy miles away. I did not see her for several months, but we wrote to each other often, and in that way, we tried to carry on our courtship until we could see each other again. Well, that is the way I met Dollie Cameron, who was to be my first wife. I will have more to say about her later. She was a faithful wife and mother in the short time she had to live, and much is due to her, though it can never be repaid by me with anything I could say or do.

Sometimes I find it very hard to go on with this story, but if I knew it would be read and appreciated by my family or anyone else, I would be glad to go on, and writing it does afford me a little pastime to keep me occupied now that I seem unable to do worthwhile work anymore. Were it not for the important things that happened in my life many years later, I think I should like to draw the line here and write a finish to it.

Mr. Atkinson's ranch was in the open country where antelope were plentiful, and it was my job to furnish the ranch with fresh meat, at least most of the time. Mr. "A" had a good hunting horse, and I would saddle up Old

Mack, grab my rifle, and go out and get an antelope. At least I got one most of the time, and on several trips, I got two. That afforded me a little recreation, while my pay went on just the same. Antelope were the only large game I ever killed, and I got to be pretty good at hunting them. They are an animal of the open country, seldom found in the mountains, and they are very swift, easily outrunning the best horse. They are also a very curious animal.

My favorite way of hunting antelope was to get an old buck alone, and then I would crawl up to where I could see him, and of course, he could see me. I would put a red handkerchief up on a stick to attract him. I would set my gun on my rest stick and just lie there and wait, and he would come a little nearer, then run away a short distance, then turn and come toward me again. We would keep on repeating this operation until he was close enough for me to get a good shot. I almost always got him with the first shot. I did not like to cripple them and have them get away because then the coyotes would get them if they were wounded very badly. Well, then I would hog dress him leaving the hide on, put him across the saddle, tie him on, and bring in the meat.

I think I have mentioned that the soil around that part of the country, as well as off toward the east of the ranch, was red. There was a large ravine that extended some distance back into the Red Hills, and in crossing this ravine with the irrigation ditch, we had to put in a siphon under the ground. Sometimes there would be a heavy rain or a waterspout would break loose on those red hills, and the red water would come down the ravine in great rolls. The flume was across the creek from the house. It so happened that one afternoon, when the folks were away, I was over there finishing up the filling in around the siphon with the team when I noticed a heavy black cloud gathering out east. It commenced to thunder and create lightning and acted almost as bad as a Kansas storm. I thought it might be a good idea for me to take the team and wagon and get back across the creek, and as the fork where I had to cross the creek was below the north of the ravine, I was afraid I would not be able to get across before the flood got there.

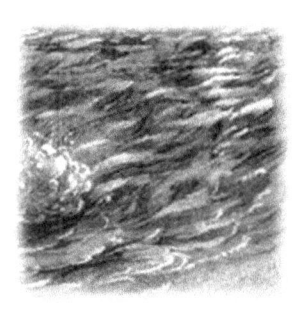

As I whipped the horse up into a run, I looked back and saw the red water coming in a great roll, with the red foam on top making it look like a river of blood. Well, I got across just ahead of the flood and drove the team out to a safe distance, then jumped off the wagon and grabbed a saddle rope I happened to have along. Just as I got to the bank of the river, I saw the largest section of our siphon approaching on the crest of the flood, and by some good chance of fortune, I managed to get my rope over one end of the thing. By taking advantage of the power of the water, I succeeded in getting it out far enough so that I could anchor it to some heavy sagebrush, thereby saving the large section of the flume. Yes, that was an exciting few minutes for me, but it was soon over, and the water went down quickly.

When the boss came home, he could cross the creek easily, and when he saw the section of siphon tied to the sagebrush, he laughed, as was his way when anything out of the ordinary took place, whether good or bad. He said when we put the thing in again, we will put it overhead, and we did, and the next flood went under it. I have had quite a bit of experience in surveying and making irrigating ditches, but I have never seen another place where it was so hard to make a ditch hold the water as it was in that red soil. We would work for days making a sidehill cut and then turn the water in, and the next morning the whole side of the ditch would be washed out. Well, I could tell of many such experiences, but I would need to be a much younger man to get them all on paper.

I could tell of the time we drove one hundred head of cattle twelve miles, ran them through a chute, and then sawed their horns off, but that would be a bloody tale. There were only three of us to do the job. I could tell of the fierce, white, man-eating stallion that was on the range there, near where I was working. He would take after a person on horseback and run them off the range. One day, I was out there looking for cattle and saw him coming as fast as he could in my direction. I got off my horse, took my rifle out of the holster, and took a few steps away from my horse. Had he not changed his mind and gone back to his bunch, he would have been a dead horse. It was against the law to have such an animal loose on the range. Not long after that, the stallion was found dead, so someone else must have done the job. I was just glad it had not been me.

I owned a beautiful young saddle horse, a bay with a white stripe down his face. He would have weighed about a thousand pounds. I called him Joy, and I think he justified the name because it was a joy to ride him. He was so gentle and kind and so full of life. And when I had some time to spare, I would saddle him up and go for a ride, which helped to drive away the monotony.

There was a fossil camp several miles down the creek from the ranch. I went there once in a while to watch them dig out the bones of those prehistoric animals. This was very interesting, as the bones were of tremendous size and caused a person to wonder what such an animal would look like if it were all together and in the flesh.

Well, I do not suppose there ever was a human being who saw one of them alive, but I would not like to meet one of them in the dark. They had to be very careful in taking them out, as the bones would crumble when the air hit them after having lain there for thousands of years. The way they did it was to work around the bones a little at a time, covering them with plaster of paris, and that would protect them from the air. Then they would crate them up and ship them to a museum in New York. Well, they were not like Ezekiel's Valley of Dry Bones, as they had to be dug out by human hands.

It was quite an undertaking, going to a place where there was not a stick of timber or any kind of shelter, and then trying to make a home and a ranch out of it in the space of two years. It required going into the hills and cutting the needed logs, poles, and fence posts. At the same time, I was looking out for about three thousand sheep and one hundred head of cattle, as well as the work stock. We also had to haul the required items and material over long distances, but somehow it was all accomplished. In that space of time, we built a house, barn, chicken house, a large and small shed, a vegetable cellar, two large sheep corrals, and several miles of fencing and irrigating ditches. I even slept in a teepee tent when it was below zero until we could live in the house.

I guess the Atkinson family must have liked me pretty well, as there were four brothers, and I did most of the work of building a house for each one of them before building one for Dollie and myself. And even after that, I was not through with building for others, for my brother Elmer and I took apart in sections and moved two houses. One of them we moved sixteen miles, and the other, twenty-seven miles, and then we put them up again and remodeled them, also before I was able to do my own work.

Meanwhile, Dollie had come home to her folks, and I would saddle up Joy every two weeks or more often and go visit her. Her father was a great talker and seemed to be under the impression that I came over just to hear him spin yarns. He also acted as if he was afraid to allow me to be alone with the girl (his daughter). All this was pretty annoying to Dollie and me, but where there is a will, there is always a way. At least Mother Cameron was on my side, and we did manage to be alone once in a while.

Well, it went on this way until just a short while before we were married. I never had a chance to ask him for his daughter's hand in marriage, until one day when Mrs. Cameron said to him, "Dad, we will have to have some spuds for dinner." He had just started on one of his long-winded stories but stopped long enough to ask me if I would like to go and see his potato cellar. I said yes, of course, hoping to get a chance to bring up the marriage idea while we were out of the house. But he just kept on telling his story, and even when he was supposed to be telling me about the cellar, he never let loose of his line of lingo long enough for me to get a word in. As I did not know when I would ever get him alone again, I finally just broke in on his yarn and said, "Dad, Dollie and I would like to get married, and we would like your consent." And he said, "If you folks are satisfied, so am I," and went right on and finished his story. I do not know to this day what the story was about as I was too much interested in something else. While I would have liked very much to have had more cooperation from my future father-in-law, that was all I got at that time.

While I am thinking about this subject, it just so happens that this very day on which I am writing this, January of 1946, would have been Dollie's and my forty-fourth wedding anniversary, were she still alive. As for Dad Cameron, when the time came that we really were going to be married, he was willing to help with making arrangements in any way he could, which I will tell about later.

Before I go any further with this part of my story, I suppose I should say a little more about the part Elmer and I took in furnishing the music for about all of the old-time dances around that community for some time. While living alone in the cabin on Cow Creek, I had finished the inlaid guitar, and it was a very beautiful instrument as well as a very fine-tuned one. Being alone so much it had given me many hours of comfort, time I spent just sitting and practicing and learning to play and sing. Meanwhile, Elmer had been going through about the same "schooling" with the violin that I was going through with the guitar, having enforced loneliness as his teacher, and we soon learned to play together. I was a fairly good singer then, and it was no problem for me to commit those songs of the time to memory. I still have most of them stored away in the same place, but I am unable to sing them anymore as my voice is no longer good. And I can still play some of them too, but not according to the modern methods of today's so-called music. My music surely would not be very popular with the "jazz hounds" of our times, but it was acceptable to the old-timers of those days, and some still like to hear me play.

Before long, Elmer and I played for our first dance, and we and our instruments became very popular. We were the only ones who got to go and have a good time and also get paid for it! That old inlaid guitar traveled many hundreds of miles, tied up in a seamless grain sack and strapped across my shoulders, while I steered my saddle horse over all kinds of roads in all kinds of weather. We sometimes went as far as forty miles just to play for a dance, and on at least one occasion, the party lasted all night. Sometimes the day would be well started before we were on our way back home.

There would always be a big feed at midnight. After everything was cleared away, the local talent would be given a chance to prove itself in songs and jigs or in anything anyone might feel inclined to do. This helped pass an hour or so and gave the dancers time to rest up and get ready for the last stage of the night's amusement. The midnight program always gave me a chance to sing my old songs. I should mention that there was no age limit at these parties. The old people went, as well as the young. If they did not care to dance, they seemed to enjoy watching the younger folks, as well as getting a chance to visit their neighbors.

I'll put in a few words here to tell about the final exit of my favorite guitar. After our wedding, Dollie and I hitched up the team and went away for a few days on a visit, and it rained just about all the time we were gone. We had left the guitar hanging on the wall, and when we got back, the house had leaked, and it had gotten soaked. The glued work all came to pieces, as that was about all it was, just pieces glued together, and that was the end of that old friend of the lonely trails. After coming to Washington state I bought a new one, the only one I ever bought and I still have, but it has never been used to play for dances. I think I have said enough now about these social parties, so I will get back to the part of the story where I left.

After completing my work at the Atkinson's, I established my headquarters in my own little homestead cabin without a floor in it, and only one small window. I had nothing more than a camp outfit to get along with. I traded my saddle horse, Joy, for a team (he was later sold to Uncle Sam as a cavalry horse for the Spanish-American War). I had a wagon, so I went back into the hills about thirty miles and started getting out logs for our new house. It was to be another log cabin, just sixteen by twenty-six feet, with three rooms to start with, logs on the inside, and a common board floor, but I must tell about getting out the logs.

Mr. Atkinson had employed a Negro by the name of Jordan to herd sheep for him for a number of years. Jordan eventually filed on a homestead back in the hills where I had cut my foot. Jordan had quit his job and had bought himself a team and outfit, and he wanted to join me in getting out logs so he could build his homestead cabin. As I had supplied his camp wagon and moved camp for him while still working for Atkinson, I had known him for several years and knew him to be a clean fellow about his body, as well as a jolly sort. He was also a good worker, although as slow as cold molasses. His black face did not bother me a bit, as I had not been raised in the South, so I told him to come along with me, and we would camp in the hills together.

So we each laid in a supply of the things we would need and took out teams. After finding a good spot close to the timber to make camp, we went to work cutting logs and hauling them out to where we could get at them with the wagons. We only cut the dead timber as the green trees were too heavy to haul that far. In that dry country, the dead trees were usually so sound that when a person struck them with the axe, they would ring like a bell. Unlike the Washington forests that keep on growing and do not seem to know when to stop, these trees died off at a certain age. That accounted for the abundance of dead trees in the area, sometimes still standing but often fallen down.

Well, those were good times for me, and when I think of them, I sometimes wish I could live them over again. I think of it as it was then, with the visions of a young life with so much to look forward to as it seemed then, as I was starting to build a home not just for me, but for the two of us and what might follow.

Well, we worked steadily and piled up the logs in the daytime and then fixed our meals and sat by the campfire at night, talking and singing songs. Jordan, like most of his color, was a fair singer and also an amusing one. When he sang songs like "*The Yellow Rose of Texas*," his whole body responded to the rhythm of the tune. As I think of the great question of our times, "What are we going to do with the Negro?" the question comes to me, "What would the world do without them?" In all my years in Wyoming, I never met but two Negroes, that is, to know them, and the other was a cowboy. On the roundup once, he let me ride his favorite horse, and that was something for him, as he was very particular about his string of horses. He was killed by a horse later on, so badly hurt that he lay on the plains and died before they found him. So ended the life of Segal George (so they say), the Negro cowboy and horsebreaker who was finally broken by a horse.

Well, when we finally got our logs out, we had to make some new roads to enable us to shorten our hauling route. This took a little while, but we were soon ready for the long haul back home, which took two days. We would go up one day, load up, then drive back several miles to a good camping place where there was good grass for the horses and a nice spring of water, and there we would spend the night. The next day, we would get back with our loads in good time to unload and get ready for the next trip.

I remember one trip, I think it was the last one, when it was getting pretty late in the fall and the weather was a little threatening. We camped in our usual place, but when I pushed back the tarpaulin the next morning to take a look around, I got a big gob of snow right in my face and down my neck. When I looked around, the ground was covered with a nice coat of new snow. Well, I dressed quietly, built the campfire, and looked after the horses. Then I called Jordan, who was completely covered with the snow, and when he pushed back the covers and stuck his black head out, he let out a yell and commenced to sing "*Roll, Jordan, Roll.*" It struck me so funny, with his black face contrasting with the white covering of snow, that I had a good laugh at the picture, and have never forgotten it. Sometimes small things live over again in our memories, while the more important things are forgotten.

Well, at last, the logs were on the ground, and then I had to make a couple of trips to sawmills for the lumber. These were long trips, about thirty-eight miles to one mill and about twenty-five miles to the other, in a different direction. So between these trips, I would work with the broadax, hewing out the logs, while the horses' rested up for the next trip. So like Nehemiah of biblical times, I built up the walls, but unlike him, I did not have a crew of willing workers. I worked alone and raised up them twenty-eight foot logs by myself. I was used to this kind of work and knew how to take advantage of it, so it was not so hard for me, but before I got through with the house, winter set in, and I had to finish it up in the cold freezing weather.

One day, when I had just got the stove set up and was getting things in shape so I could live in the house, who should come riding up but my prospective father-in-law! He had come all the twenty-five miles in the cold to help us make arrangements for the wedding. I got ready and went back with him the next day.

We set the date for the twenty-ninth of January. The wedding was to be at their place, with the usual dance and everything that was customary for these occasions. As I had a friend who was a justice of the peace, it was decided that he would officiate. I had promised him that if I ever got married, I would let him perform the ceremony, and I made good on my promise to him. There were about sixty-five grown people who came to our wedding, from as far away as about forty-five miles, and they danced all night (it was too cold for the children). Strange as it may sound, I helped to furnish some of the music for my own wedding! It was a hard winter and the snow was piled high in drifts. Since the Cameron home was about a thousand feet higher in elevation than our place and the road there very much worse, I built a light sled just for the occasion. That trip was about all it was ever used for.

The next day, we loaded up all the bride's earthly possessions, as well as the bride, and put in some hot stones to keep our feet warm. We started the twenty-five miles home, and in places I suppose we went over snowdrifts (with crusted tops) that were ten to twelve feet deep. The weather was around thirty-five below zero, day and night, but I had a fellow staying at the place to feed the cattle while I was away, and he had the house warm for us when we arrived. This was Dollie's introduction to her new home, which was also her last home upon this earth. Thereon hangs a sad tale, which I will tell in part as I go along.

As our herd of cattle was few in number and we could not afford to live off of them, it was necessary for me to take a job on the outside once in a while when the opportunity came along. I was away from home in the daytime while working at these jobs, and it was pretty lonely for my young wife, but she never complained much about it. We were both working with the one thought in mind that someday we would be independent of this outside work and able to put all our time into building up our ranch and herd of cattle.

So we filed on some more desert land and bet Uncle Sam a dollar and twenty-five cents an acre that we could make a go of it. I dug out ditches, grubbed out the sagebrush, and seeded the ground with timothy and redtop, and sowed oats and barley for stock feed. There were also some native grasses. It was not long until I was making the desert bloom, not as the rose, but in shades of green. I will say, it was a great satisfaction to see the old gray sagebrush give way to the beautiful green of the waving fields or meadows, especially when you knew it had been brought about by your own special efforts. So it was that the cold cheerless winter passed away, and spring came with flowers to "deck sweet May," as the old song goes. And the place that had been rejected as not worth filing on, in time, became the best ranch on the creek. But now I'm getting ahead of my story again. To make this story real, I must tell some of the bad, along with the good.

When we were first married, my wife would kneel by the bed and say her prayers before going to sleep, and one of the saddest memories of my life is that she had no help from me. Rather, I made light of it, and she soon neglected her prayers as far as I could tell. And although the Lord has forgiven my sins and removed the condemnation, that one mistake in my life will always be regretted, for although I did it ignorantly, there was no cause for me to hinder her in her devotions to God. Had I known what I do today of my Savior's love, I would have knelt beside her. The two of us would have given the Lord his place in our lives, and things would have been so much better for us. But like many people, I forgot the real God and made the work of my hands and my ambitions the only God I knew.

My wife and I were together as much as was reasonably possible, and we had a favorite place on top of a large boulder we could very easily climb up on from one side. From this observation point we could see all over the ranch, could even see the water running in the ditches far below us. We also had a view of the outside plains for a distance of about fifteen miles. Some nice, sunny afternoons when the work was done up, we would go up there and sit and dream and just look around. Well, such hours were never wasted and I can remember them with pleasure. I think it is a good thing for anyone to just forget the work and trials of life once in a while, get away from it all, and think of something else. Like one time when we took the team and drove about twelve miles to a good trout stream, where we stopped over for two nights. We caught a lot of trout, and even though we salted them down, they all spoiled, but we had the fun of catching them so it was worth the trip.

I think it was the first summer after our marriage when my father came out from Denver to spend a few weeks with us, as he was in poor health. They thought the change of climate might improve his health, which it seemed to do. Anyway, he had a good time, and he and Dollie seemed to hit it off pretty well. I was glad for this as it was the last time I ever saw my father, as he died soon afterward in October of that year.

Our first baby was born before her time as a result of an accident Dollie had in crossing the creek. It was a girl, and we called her Edith May for my oldest sister. The next year, our second girl baby was born dead. So in a little clearing out around the point of rocks not far from the house and surrounded by large sagebrush, we buried our first hopes of a family. This sadness came to us when Dollie was still very young, and we began to wonder if we would ever have a child who lived, and of course, we were pretty badly broken up about it.

About this time, the party who had bought my place on the creek below, about a mile away, sold out to a large cattle company. I had built a store several years before for Mr. Cameron, and the new owners wished to run it. They asked me to move a large log house for them from a ranch about six miles away to my old place then rebuild it to be the new home of a man and wife they had hired from the East to manage the store for them. The man had tuberculosis and thought the high climate might cure him. So I took the job of moving and rebuilding the house, even though it was about an all-winter's job and a very cold one. It would give us a chance to make some money so we could get along without having to sell off some of our cattle. Well, of course, Dollie had to stay home alone all day and it was very lonely for her. She would watch for me to come home every evening just before dark.

One such evening I was later than usual. I had come upon a bad blizzard, and in order to keep out of the wind, I had followed the creek along by the willows where it was more sheltered. That took a little longer than usual, so when I finally got home I found Dollie crying and just about ready to head out to hunt for me. She thought I was lost in the blizzard. Well, you would not wonder at her anxiety if you knew that country as we did. There were people frozen to death there very often for being lost in a blizzard, and I will likely tell about such a case soon.

That winter was a hard one, and we did not have very much hay to feed the cattle and could not buy any. In order to keep them from starving, I separated the strongest from the weakest, putting the stronger ones out on the hills to rustle their living while I fed the weaker ones. In that way, we only lost one cow, but they were a hard-looking bunch when the snow finally started to melt off, and they could get some feed on the range. After that winter's experience, I made up my mind to never go into another winter without plenty of hay. I succeeded pretty well in keeping my vow, for I never lost any more cattle from starvation. I will never forget that winter, as I spent so much time out on the hills, trying to keep those cattle out where they could get enough feed to keep themselves alive. When I finally got home from riding all day in the cold, sometimes my face would be so covered with ice, I could hardly breathe. I wore a heavy mustache in those days, or at least it was heavy, when all that ice was on it!

Not far from the house, I had built a shop for a place to work, and also to store my tools and farm machinery. It was about sixteen by twenty-four feet. It had a chest filled with all kinds of carpenter's tools I had acquired when I worked in the factory in Denver, valued at about 250 dollars. Connected with the shop, I had built a handmade windmill, and then I got a circular saw and rigged up an outfit for cutting wood, using the gearing of an old mowing machine. On windy days I would use some of this free power, so plentiful in Wyoming, to cut wood. I even rigged up a cylinder for threshing grain on a very small scale.

One time, we invited some friends over to listen to our new phonograph and have dinner with us. At the time, I had a nice large rick of stovewood cut and split up, enough to last a year or two. It was a very windy day, and when our friends were leaving, one of them said, "Bob, your shop has burned down!" Sure enough, I looked out to see that my shop and tools, the windmill, and all of my farm machinery were now nothing but a smoking bed of coals.

The wind had made such a roaring sound blowing through the hills that we had not even noticed the roaring of the fire. We managed to save most of the stovewood, but that was all. Well, that was a pretty bad jolt as most of what was lost had to be replaced, and there was no insurance. We were thankful it did not get the barn and what hay was left, or harm the horses and stock that were in the barn, which would have happened had we not found it out when we did.

In saving the wood, we had also saved the barn and all it contained. I never rebuilt the shop, but I did rebuild the windmill in a little larger size and in a better location. It cut most of our wood as long as we lived there. Later on, I sold it to a man who was going to set it up out on the open plains where the wind really blows. I have often wondered if it was able to withstand the extra draft.

The couple managing the store had just gotten things in shape to carry on their business when the woman contracted a case of the flu. It then developed into quick TB (tuberculosis), and she died from it. This was the same thing that her husband had come out West to get cured of. So I nailed up a sort of shipping casket to put the body in, and Mr. Matheson, the friend I spoke of in an earlier part of my story, took the body all the way to Laramie City. He drove seventy-five miles by team at night and all alone. I mention this because of the wonderful help he was to me later on under similar circumstances. He told me later how lonely he felt on that long drive at night, with a dead person riding in the back of the open-spring wagon. So it was in those days before the automobile came into use. Someone had to deprive himself of the comforts of home and venture out into the cold night to help out in a case like this, and it seemed that more often than not, that person was Bill Matheson.

Only a short time later, a couple of men left Rock River for the store, with a four-horse team and a load of supplies. A blizzard came up, and they got stuck in a snowdrift about twelve miles from their destination. They turned their horses loose, started out on foot toward the hills where the store was, and got lost. Night came on, and the older man gave out and froze to death. The younger man made it through to the hills and managed to get underneath the shelter of a rock, where he waited until daylight. He then found his way to one of the neighboring ranches.

Word was sent to me, and I went down to see the man. He was pretty badly frozen, but he was able to tell us about the other fellow, who he said was dead by the time he had left him. We organized a party to go out and find the body, but the storm was so bad, we could not face it and had to wait until the next day. By morning, when the storm had broken up and the sun had come out, we got together a small band, with a Mr. Tom Garrett who had a team and sled. The rest of us rode our horses, and the men had a dog with them that belonged to Garrett, which they were bringing out for him. The dog led us most of the time to where we found the frozen man. There he was, out on a high ridge, his back to the wind and the snow all drifted around him. Only his face was showing; the bright, cold light of the sun shining full upon his face. Well, we put him on the sled and took him to the ranch, and for the second time within a few weeks, I was nailing up a rough box for a body. We put him in it just as he was to be sent to the city. Well, the younger man lost some fingers and toes and a part of one ear (I think, they said), but otherwise, he got all right again.

I should say something about the heavy loss of sheep that often occurred in those blizzards. Sometimes, great herds of them would be caught out there on the plains, and there was nothing the herder could do but just let them drift with the storm and follow them until the storm let up. Often, they would try to cross a washout filled with snow, and they would go down, the whole herd piling right in on top of them. Many would be smothered or trampled to death in this way. After the storm was over, a person could easily trace the course of the drifting herd by the dead bodies strewn along the trail. Well, I was in the cattle business, and cattlemen did not like sheep, or—as a rule—sheepmen. Still, it was a sad picture to look at and somebody had to suffer the loss.

Well, the long winter ended at last, and the snow commenced to melt. As soon as I could get at the roots of the sagebrush, I started in with the grubbing hoe Elmer had made for me out of the spring of an old mowing machine seat. It was made with two bits, and I always kept it sharp. I would grub, pile up, and burn it at a rate of about two acres a week, and I did the burning at night. Dollie would often go out and watch the fires. I strung them from one pile to the other, and the flames would go straight up into the still night air. I guess it reminded me somewhat of the Kansas prairie fires after the wind had gone down at night and the wall of fire would go straight up into the air. It made a pretty picture; at least, it seemed so to me.

During the summer I am telling about, I decided to make a special effort and hired a man for a few days to help me sow about twenty-five acres of oats and barley. I wanted to be sure that the cattle would not go hungry. When it was all nicely headed out, it was about the nicest prospect I had ever seen. The man who had helped me came around one day, and after dinner, I took him out to see my nice field of grain. I had heard it thunder several times and did not pay much attention to it at first, but when I finally looked back toward the north, over the top of the mountain was a heavy black cloud. It was coming fast, and I told my friend we better get back to the house or we might get wet.

I should say that when a thunderstorm breaks over the mountains in Wyoming, it is not an all-day affair as it sometimes is in Kansas, but it comes in a hurry, and so it was this time. We had not yet made it to the house before it started in and the hail and rain came down in great sheets. In less than twenty minutes, the ground was white with hail and piled up in places. As soon as it had stopped, we went out to see what it had done to the crop. Where the grain had stood, there was just a white covering of hail. And so another one of my earthly goods was pounded into the earth in just a few minutes. It came up again, but never amounted to much.

As I have grown older, I have learned that it does not pay to put too much faith in earthly things, for they are very uncertain. I guess the Lord was trying to teach me that lesson then, but I did not know enough to profit by it. He has said, "You shall have no other gods before Me." Although it is our duty to raise the grain and even to enjoy seeing it grow and to take great pleasure in the harvest, when we put it ahead of our Creator, it becomes a false god and stands between us and the real God.

In thinking about some of the things that happened over the years I was in Wyoming, I find there are several I have forgotten to mention that might be interesting. I will reach back a little to the time I was "batching it" in the old cabin on the creek. As I have mentioned before, I raised quite a few potatoes and sometimes had to haul them to the towns along the railroad in order to find a sale for them. Then I often found the market already well-supplied.

It so happened that Elmer was raising vegetables and had some to sell, so we decided to make a trip together to the coal mining town of Carbon, about forty-five miles from my ranch. He loaded up what he had to sell and drove up to my place one evening. After staking his horses out on the meadow near the house, we worked on getting ready to start out on our trip the next day. But when Elmer went out to get his team the next morning, he found his best horse down. She was still alive, but the wolves had eaten a great hole in her back parts and he had to shoot her. The poor kid was so discouraged he did not know what to do as that left him without a team.

Well, we put what he had on top of my load and started out, and when we got to Medicine Bow, we thought we would lighten up the load by trying to sell some of the spuds there. We drove up to a house and asked the old lady who lived there if she would like to buy a sack of spuds, and I will never forget the shock I got when she said, "It's Sunday." Well, we just pulled out of town to a good camping place, stayed over until the next day, and took the lesson that the old Christian lady had taught us in just two words with the best grace we could. To think that two-word sermon came from one of the toughest little towns in Wyoming at that time. We went to Carbon the next day and found the town well supplied, but succeeded in trading our load to the commissary store in exchange for groceries and things we needed, along with some things we did not need.

When we got back home, I set a trap and caught the gray wolf that had tried to eat the horse alive. It was the largest one I had ever seen. When I saw him in the trap, I took a club and went out to kill him, but when he came toward me showing his teeth, and I saw I only had him by his toes, I changed my mind and went back and got the rifle. I guess he must have thought I looked like the back end of a horse.

On another trip, I took a load of potatoes weighing about twenty-seven hundred pounds to Hanna, another coal mining town about fifty miles from home. I found the same conditions there, the market was flooded and nobody wanting to buy. But when I told some folks that I would trade for sacks, the kids came running from all directions with bundles of sacks. I needed the sacks for my crop of spuds and soon got rid of the potatoes in that way, but that was a long way to go to get this kind of a deal. Unfortunately, the worst was yet to come, for just as I had gotten rid of my last sack of spuds, the heavens let loose with hail and rain. It was coming down in torrents that not only soaked me to the skin but wet my bedding through, and the sacks as well. As I pulled out of town, it started to snow, and before I could get very far on my way, the ground was white and it was still coming down.

When I got out in the Greenwood Country, the horses commenced to slip and slide, and the wagon wheels rolled up the mud so badly, I had to knock the brake blocks out to keep them clear of the mud. I had figured on getting back to Medicine Bow that night, about twelve miles down the road, but I saw that the horses could never make it. When I came to a place where there was some grass, I pulled out of the road and unhitched the horses, tying one out and leaving the other loose. There was nothing to make a fire with, so I got out my wet bed, rolled it out, and crawled into it, wet clothes and all. I can say truthfully that that was the most miserable night I ever spent in my life, barring extreme illness, as it kept right on snowing and melting and leaking down through the sacks (my bed was on the ground under the wagon). I may as well have been sleeping out in the open.

The next day, I got to Medicine Bow by a little after noon and put my team in the barn, got some things from the store to eat, and sat by the store heater trying to get dried out a little. When bedtime came, I slept in my wet bedding another night, but in the barn this time. Well, I was pretty badly discouraged that night, about half sick and feeling like I never wanted to see another potato, but since I had over twenty tons at home yet to get rid of, there was no quitting place. So I made a deal with the store there at Medicine Bow to take all I could deliver at a very low price, and I was to take half of that price in trade, so this was only the beginning. I think I delivered about twelve tons over that thirty-five-mile distance before the weather got too cold to continue hauling them.

It took me till after dark to get home the next day, as the roads were still so slippery and bad. I remember one trip where I camped overnight about twelve miles from home, and one of my horses got away in the night. I had to go all the way back to the ranch to get him, and by the time I got back to the wagon, I had to stay there another night before going on. And that is just a good example of how we often progress in life, getting exactly nowhere no matter how hard we try.

There was another time, previous to when Elmer had lost his horse, when he was doing some assessment work on some mine prospects back in the mountains, about twenty-five miles northwest of my place. Elmer had taken his team up there and camped out, and while he was doing his work, the horses got away from him and came home, leaving him afoot. He sent me a letter asking me to bring them back, as he was through with the work and wanted to pack up and come home. He also sent a chart of the area he was in so I could find him, as I was not very well acquainted with that part of the country. So one morning, I got the horses and started out. When I came to the place where the chart showed I should turn off the main road and follow some wagon tracks a certain distance, a large band of sheep was milling around and I could not find the right place, at least where I thought it should be. I hunted in different places without results, until it commenced to get dark.

I had just about given up for the night when I saw a campfire to the north that appeared to be only a short ways off. As I had already tied out the horse I was riding and turned the other one loose, I thought I would just walk over to the camp and get Elmer, then come back and get the horses after I had something to eat. I had not eaten a thing since early that morning. I started hiking toward the fire, calling once in a while, but could get no answer, so I thought he must be asleep. I kept going until I came to what is known as LaBonte Canyon, looking like a great black cleft in the earth, which it was. Although there was no moon at the time, I could still see the campfire appearing to be just across the canyon on about a level with where I was standing. Since it was a long way back to the horses, I decided to try to cross the canyon, scrambling over rock and through brush and trees for several hundred feet.

Finally, I reached the bottom and waded the creek, and then I tackled the climb up the other side, thinking when I got to the top, I would surely be right close to Elmer's camp. But when I finally reached the top of the canyon wall, the fire was still a long way off. By yelling loud and long, I finally got an answer, which sounded like it came from over in Montana somewhere. Steering each other with our calls, I kept pushing onward until we finally came together in a thicket of small timber. He then led me to his camp and fixed something for me to eat.

When I told him where the horses were, as near as I could describe the place, he said we would just leave them there until tomorrow, for it was several miles away. I was just talking to Elmer the other day, and he said he never did understand how I got across LaBonte Canyon in the dark that night. I told him I did not know myself, for it would have been a task even in daylight. We got the horses the next day by going around on the road, and then we packed up and pulled back to the ranch.

I will now continue my story, starting in the summer of 1904, the summer that Pearl was born. As we had already lost two babies, we decided that Dollie should go home to her folks where she would be close to a good midwife and stay there until her baby was born and she was strong enough to come home. So it was there at the Cameron home, on the twenty-seventh of August, when Pearl was born. When I heard about it, I rode the twenty-five miles before noon to see her. She looked pretty small to me, but they said she was healthy and that Dollie was getting along fine too.

Cameron log cabin near Marshall, Wyoming where Pearl, Robert and Dollie's first child to survive was born in 1904

Dollie was very happy, of course, and so was I. When she was finally able to come home with the baby, things seemed to be different around the old place. I suppose we both felt that we had something more to keep us busy and make life worthwhile. As the weeks and months passed by and Pearl grew into a strong, healthy baby and commenced to notice things and smiled once in a while, it was very special. I guess we were just like all other parents. What is the use of me trying to tell about what followed? The fact that she is still alive and has children of her own who are almost grown is enough to tell of the final happy results.

Dollie was very much afraid of lightning, I suppose owing to the fact that her older sister had been killed and her mother crippled for life by lightning in Kansas when she was just a little girl. When a bad thunderstorm came up, she would go into the bedroom, pull down the blinds, and hide herself away until the storm had passed. No amount of argument on my part would ever cure her of that fear. Taking population into account, Wyoming was the worst place I ever saw for people being killed by lightning, as nearly every summer there would be someone killed. Of course, that did not help Dollie's case any.

There was a young Englishman who lived just above us on the creek, who was what they called a "remittance man." That is, he was one of those young fellows who was given five hundred dollars by his father and sent to that part of the country to learn ranching. It almost always happened that somebody would beat them out of the money, and they would be left without a dollar until they could convince their dads with some kind of hard-luck tale and get some more money. Well, this young fellow was no exception to the rule, but somehow, he managed to become engaged to a fine young lady schoolteacher in our community.

I suppose she thought she was marrying an English title and that she could most likely feed on that somehow. Anyway, this fellow had a horse and top buggy, and it was his habit to drive to town, that is Laramie City, once in a while, and he would be gone several days at a time. I have mentioned before that when one of us went out for the mail, we would bring back the mail for everyone along the route as far as our place. On the day I am thinking about, I had been out and collected the mail, and when Mr. "T", as we will call him, came down, I gave him a letter that had an English postmark on it. After he had read it, he threw up his hands and hollered, "Hurrah, the old bugger is dead at last!" When we found out the good news, it was to the effect that his rich uncle had died in Australia and had left him quite a sum of money. Of course, he was a rich man for a while.

One fine summer morning, he pulled out for Laramie, and we missed him for a week or more. We were wondering why he did not show up again back at the ranch. Then we got word that his body had been found on the road, where it had lain for nearly a week. He had been killed by lightning. Well, I just reach into the side pocket, as it were, and pull out one of these little stories because it sometimes brings a good lesson from personal experience and also is of sufficient interest to make things readable or entertaining.

Putting up the hay crop was quite a job, as it was hard to get help out in the country. Most of the men who could have worked in the hayfields liked to hang around close to a saloon or somewhere else where they could blow their money. So I built myself a stacker out of some timbers and small poles that I got from the woods. Outside of a rope, some pulleys, and a few bolts, it did not cost much but just work. I had been brought up on that, and did not mind the working part a bit. As I had the sweep and a good mower and rake, I was all hooked up for business.

So in the summer, Pearl was a year old, I think it was, I started putting up a large crop of hay. My neighbor sent me up a couple of men who, he said, wanted to work, but after they had shown me they were not much good, I let them go and went at it alone with the old white team. All I needed was someone to hook the stacker rope for me when I was stacking. Dollie would come out with the baby and sit in the shade of the stack with her needlework, and when I came in with a sweep load of hay, she would hook the rope for me. Then I would pull it up on the stack with the team, and by mowing and raking part of the hay and stacking the other part, we made pretty good progress. As the haying season is pretty long there, I managed in this way to get it all in the stack in good time.

There was one year we put up 160 tons in this way. About 50 tons of it had to be hauled with the wagon and racked to the stackyards at the barn. What was put up in the field with the stacker had to be fenced in with a pole fence, where it could be fed out right on the meadow from where it was grown, and in that way, conserve the fertility of the soil. I had learned the lesson by our first experience that selling the crop off the ground, year after year, will finally deplete the soil. Well, the hay crop was not all we had to look after. I was still raising potatoes, and they had to be dug up in time and stored away in a potato cellar where they would not freeze during the long cold winter.

At around the time I have been writing about, the handwriting had begun to show on the wall that there was trouble ahead for the cattlemen. There had begun to be more money in sheep than there was in cattle, and the continuing menacing presence of the big sheep baron was felt. They brought in large bands of sheep, sometimes from outside the country, and stole the range that rightly belonged to the small cattle raisers, even in some cases going through their fences to get to the range. At least one man I knew became so bitter against the sheepmen that he got together a party to go out and move a sheep camp out of a cattleman's pasture. It got to the point where the sound of a sheep bell caused a fellow to look for his gun.

The range where I had always put my cattle in the summer was being threatened by sheep coming in, and to those who do not know it, I would like to say that cattle will just about starve before they will eat the grass that sheep have run over. I am telling this to show the condition of things the last few years we spent in Wyoming. With the constant threat of trouble brewing, my peace of mind was not what it should have been. There had been more than one sheep-and-cattle war already, and I did not care to have a part in one.

So both Dollie and I began to plan to leave that part of the country and go to someplace where it was a little more civilized, but as yet, we did not feel that we had enough so that we could turn it into money to start up somewhere else. So we kept hanging on, even though we could have sold at a fair price. Dollie had always wanted to live where there was plenty of fruit, so I even made a trip into southern Idaho to look for a new location for us. I spent a week looking around, but nothing came of it except that I spent some of our hard-earned money on a railroad ticket. About this time, something happened that caused one sheepman to move out and things eased up a little, so we decided to stick around for a while longer.

Then Fred was born, and we had two children to look out for, and I guess we did a fair job of it, for he is still going strong and has two babies of his own now. Fred was born in the old log house on Cow Creek on July 21, 1906, which will make him forty years old next July. Well, when he was big enough to play around out in the yard, Pearl thought it was her job to look after him when their mother was busy, and she did a pretty good job of it for her age.

I had just gotten a new team of Percherons, not fully broken yet, and I had them hitched up to a brand new Peter Schuttler wagon. I guess they were a little proud of the outfit and were showing off, and it was all I could do to handle them when I came around the house, and there right in my path was little Fred playing in the dirt.

PETER SCHUTTLER, CHICAGO.

Farm Wagon with Schuttler Brake.

I heard a screech and Pearl came like a streak from behind the house, grabbed the little fellow and pulled him back, regardless of her own danger. Of course, I had seen him and he was safe, but she did not think so. Pearl was a very active child for her age, as she could walk and talk at nine months, and she still knows how.

I had bought this team together with another team of young mares, and they were all from the same sire and all sorrels with white faces. I had paid 630 dollars for the four, and they were a beautiful outfit of horses. I never lost any money on them, for when I came West, I sold them for 775 dollars. One of the old gray team had taken sick and died, and I had to have another team, so I bought a good one. I am sure that in the long run, it is cheapest to get the best, if one can afford it.

About this time, I decided to sell our mixed bunch of cattle, about 145 heads, as I had been offered a good price for them and wanted to just run steers. I also sold some of the hay, and after paying up a few debts, put the money where I could easily get to it when I wanted it. I thought I had made a good deal but found out later I had made a big mistake, as the old bunch of stock was well-settled and would not leave their range unless driven off, while the cattle I brought in from outside would stray away. It would have been very hard to keep track of them, but as things turned out, I never got a chance to put this problem to the test, for reasons that you will understand later on. My last shipment of beef steers was made from Arin Junction, Wyoming and consisted of twenty-four head of three-year-old steers, which brought us something over thirteen hundred dollars. We had planned to use part of this money to fix up our home and make it a little more comfortable, but those plans did not fully work out as we had figured, which I shall try to show later on.

On December 1, 1908, our last baby was born, Robert J. Jr., as Dollie would have him named. He was a big husky baby, and everything was looking all right for us as far as raising a family was concerned. Things were pretty lively and noisy now for us, and we both had plenty to do to keep us from getting lonesome. About this time, Doll's father and mother sold out and moved to Washington State to live, and later, her younger brother also left Wyoming. Of course, she missed seeing her mother and family quite a bit. I am sure that if it had not been for those three little fellows, it would have been lonely indeed, as she could not get out with me so much anymore.

Dollie's oldest brother had died previous to the time her folks left Wyoming, and she had told me on several occasions that she was not going to live long, but I tried to make her believe that it was just her imagination. I could not seem to get it out of her mind, as she had had a dream of seeing her brother who was dead, and that she was going to be with him before long.

Well, it worried me quite a bit to have her feel that way, as I had known people who had had premonitions of things that later came to pass, but I did not wish to let her know I was worried about her. I tried to cheer her up and even scolded her a little for allowing those thoughts to enter her mind, so she did not say much more about it and things went along as usual until the fall of 1909.

I was busy hauling lumber and material to fix up the house, and I bought her brother's herd of white-faced steers and was fixing up for winter. She seemed in the best of health, but she complained of a pain in her side several times. Then just when winter had set in, in earnest, she got badly sick one night. I sent word to Elmer, and he came up and took the big team and crossed those forty-five miles of plains at night and in a blizzard to get to Rock River. Then he sent to Laramie for a doctor, another forty miles by train (there was no telephone out our way at that time). Well, it was thirty-six hours before Elmer got back with the doctor, and he pronounced it a case of advanced appendicitis.

He could not operate, so we had to send for another surgeon, and she died before this doctor got well on the way, only five days after she had taken down with it. So quickly were the three babies left without a mother, and little Robert had not yet been weaned when she got sick. He was just one year and seven days old, and Pearl and Fred were a few months over five and three years, respectively. Well, if there ever was a time in my life I needed God's help, it was in a time like that, but I was nothing but a lost soul and God was a stranger to me. I had no one to look to for comfort and help but a few friends, and they did not know the way any better than I did, but as far as human beings were concerned, they did all they could to help me and the children.

I shall never forget their kindness, especially my brother Elmer who made two trips across the plains to Rock River and back in the worst kind of weather, and also made a temporary casket to ship the body to Laramie in. I shall never forget Mrs. M. A. Garrett, who took care of Robert while I was away to the funeral, and Mrs. Read, who cared for all of the children until my sister Edith came from the

East. And last but not least, I must mention my old friend, Bill Matheson, who came in the next morning when I was at a loss to know what to do. He just took charge of arranging things and getting the body to the railroad, and he also took care of the funeral arrangements after we got there, of course according to my wishes.

I shall never forget that long cold drive across the forty-five miles of drifting snow, with Mr. Matheson driving the team. I was sitting there with him and the body of my wife in the rear part of the light-spring wagon. He was driving one of my young mares that had never been hitched up before to the best of my knowledge, and she just made the trip like an old, well-broken horse. The weather was so bad that nobody went from the hills but just us two, and I was afraid there would not be anyone at the funeral in Laramie. To my great surprise and satisfaction, I had more friends in the city than I had thought.

The news of Dollie's death had preceded us, and there were many offers of help and sympathy, as well as many flowers. I shall never forget how, when I was in a store that morning, a strange lady came up to me and asked me if I was the person who had lost his wife. Then she introduced herself to me and offered to sing at the funeral, and she was a beautiful singer, in more ways than one. Then there was my old friend from my younger days, who had made the bicycle trip with me over the pass to Grand Lake. He had since gone into business in Laramie, and he was very kind and helpful to me. Well, we laid her to rest beside her brother in the cemetery there in Laramie, and since then, another brother has joined them there. Out of a family of six children, there is only one left.

The hardest part of all was to go back to the motherless children and to try to explain to them why their mother did not come back. But I will not burden those who may read this story with a long, drawn-out account of the many difficulties that were mine at that time. Rather, I will try to tell more about how they were solved, at least in part. I had written Dollie's only sister, May, who lived at North Park, Colorado, and asked her if she would take care of Robert until I could be in better shape somehow to take care of them all myself. As she was going out to Washington to visit her folks that winter, she came by and took him with her on the trip. I also wrote to my sister Edith, who was coming west anyway to get married, to ask her to come and stay with me for a while and help me until I could find a better way out (which she did).

In that way, I was free more or less to do the work I had planned to do on the house. As I had the material on the ground, I thought it best to go on with it, not only for the good of the place, but also for myself as well, as I had even then found out that the best way to cure sorrow is to keep busy at something worthwhile. In the meantime, my neighbor Mr. Hall had told me of 160 head of yearling steers that could be bought for twenty dollars a head, saying that if I could take 100 of them, he would take the other 60. As I had plenty of hay to feed them, I thought I would go with him the sixty miles to see them. When we got there, we found them to be a fine bunch of mixed whitefaces, so we bought them, drove them home, and divided them up, and then for the balance of the winter, I had plenty to do.

Well, this Mr. Flake Hall was a pretty good friend of mine, and I will always remember one thing he said to me on our long 120-mile ride when—I am afraid—I was burdening him somewhat with my troubles, I told him that I had a notion to sell out and leave the country. He said, "No matter where you go, you cannot run away from your troubles." And how true I have found those words to be. If you can't stay put and live them down, you can never go away and leave them, for they will surely follow you wherever you go, at least the kind of troubles I had on my hands at that time.

Well, I went ahead and finished up the house, somewhere near the way we had figured on it, and in the meantime, May came back from Washington with little Robert. He was growing fast and looking fine, but for a while, he did not wish to have anything to do with me. It hurt quite a bit, but that was just another dose of the bitter medicine I had been taking. I just swallowed it, hoping it would have the desired effect later on, which it did. At Laramie later on, when May was on her way home, she had to wait most of the day for her train to pull out. I just sat in the car seat and played with Robert almost the whole time, and he just crawled all over me and hugged me, and we had such a good time. I am glad it was that way, for although I did not know it at the time, that was the last time I was to see him for over nineteen years. I will try to tell of that meeting later on in my story.

I will now gradually draw the curtain on the actions and scenes of over seventeen years of my life in Wyoming as I soon sold all my stock and most of the equipment to Mr. Hall and rented him the ranch for three years. On the invitation of Dollie's father and mother, I prepared to take Pearl and Fred out to Washington for what I thought was a visit, but instead, turned out to be a permanent change to a new location and a very different kind of business. Before I leave this chapter of my life, I wish to pay a word of tribute to a few old friends and associates from that time, such as T. S. Garrett and his wife. Mrs. Mary Garrett, although she was born in England, became the first woman justice of the peace in the United States. She also helped to bring at least two of my children into the world as a midwife. Also, Mrs. Lizzie Atkinson who was always so kind to me during the years I worked for her family on the Red Desert, along with her husband, Felix, who has already gone across to the other range, and his brothers George and Jim, whom I worked with and neighbored with for so many years. But what is the use in checking up on them as I find they are mostly all gone to (I hope) a better world. Anything I could say would not do them any good now, either here or in the hereafter.

And there, crossing the little bridge in front of the Wyoming house, was where I last saw my mother as she came out to visit us the year before Dollie died. There, by a strange act of fate, I bid goodbye for the last time to both Father and Mother. For I never saw either of them again after they waved goodbye and crossed the bridge over Cow Creek in front of the old log house just a year ago.

This was also the place where Fred and Robert were born and where their mother bid them goodbye, also for the last time. Now Father rests in the old soldier's cemetery near Denver, Colorado, and Mother is buried in Newberg, Oregon, not so far from our present home.

Starting Over in Washington

Edith and I packed up what things we thought we might need and we took the train at Rock River for Laramie. Now Pearl and Fred were to have their first train ride, and I suppose I thought of those two green boys who had taken their first train ride down in Kansas so many years before. When we got to Laramie that evening, we went to the hotel and got our rooms for the night and had our supper. Then we thought we would walk around a while and see the town. Out in front of a moving picture theater was a brass band all ready to strike up a tune, so we thought we would stop and listen to the music.

Well, as they often do, the brass band started up with a sudden crash of drums and everything that goes with it, and Fred jumped straight up and looked pretty badly scared. But as the music smoothed down and took on a sort of rhythm, he commenced to sway from one foot to the other, in good time with the music, keeping it up for quite a while. I never saw two little kids get more out of music than they seemed to get out of that brass band. Then we went into the show, and they also saw their first movie, but they were all the silent kind in those days. All one had to do was look and not listen.

The next morning, we got our tickets, Edith for Salt Lake City, and I for Portland, Oregon. When we got to Ogden, the man who was to become my brother-in-law, Charlie Hone, met us there and took us to Salt Lake City where we spent most of the day looking around. As it was Sunday, he took us to the Mormon Tabernacle, where we heard the great organ and also heard the world-famous choir sing. And then the children and I bid Edith and her "would become" goodbye and left them to their fate while we took the train for Portland.

That was a hard trip on the little children, for they were tired from trailing around the Salt Lake City streets in the hot sun, and although I had bought my ticket subject to Pullman privileges, there was no Pullman couch on the train, so I was compelled to bed them down on a seat. This way, they could sleep while I watched them to keep them from rolling off onto the floor. Pearl got sick, and I had a hard time of it all the way to Portland. A cranky woman came along and asked me where their mother was. I told her, and after that, she was a little more human and tried to help me a little by combing Pearl's hair. Some of the other women softened up then too, and where I had been getting plenty of suspicious looks from them, they commenced to show a little sympathy in their attitude, and that helped quite a bit.

It was late in the evening of the twentieth of June 1910 that we arrived in Portland. We took a bus to a hotel, got a room and cleaned up, and then went out to a restaurant and got our supper. After supper, I thought I would lead the children around a block or two, and let them get a glimpse of the big city. We came to a place where the Salvation Army was playing and singing on a street corner, and as I was reaching into my pocket to get some change to give them, a cop came along and told me to get along and stop blocking the street. As there was quite a crowd gathered there doing the same thing I was, I just thought that maybe I did not belong on the streets of Portland with my little family. So I took them back to the hotel and put them to bed where all good children should be at that time of night. A good night's sleep after such a long tiresome trip was just what we needed, and after we had breakfast the next morning, we boarded the streetcar for Vancouver.

As the car approached the Columbia River and crossed the old trestle, I thought I had never seen so much water, which was true. The river was at flood stage at the time. Then we went over on the ferry and into the city of Vancouver and the state of Washington, little dreaming that it would be our abiding place for so many years. My father-in-law came in and brought us out with a horse and rig. I thought we had landed in paradise, as everything was so green and beautiful compared to what I had been accustomed to seeing. The air smelled so fresh and cool after so many years in the desert. For the time, I thought that it would be a good place for us to live. Although Dad and Mother Cameron did all they could to make us feel at home, for me there was something lacking and I would get pretty lonely at times. Although I traveled around some to see the country, I was not satisfied, as I found that what Mr. Hall had said to me awhile back was true. My troubles had followed me.

Cherries were just getting ripe when we arrived in Felida, and I had the pleasure of climbing what was called "the largest cherry tree in the world" at that time, and filling myself up, as the saying goes. As the children and I had never before in our lives had all the fruit we wanted, we overdid it and ate too much. We all got sick and had to go to the doctor to get fixed up, and then Pearl commenced to break out in sores and was in a bad way for a while.

And then I took the old folks and the children on a trip to the ocean beaches, and we all (except Dad Cameron) saw the ocean for the first time. I have never tired of looking at the ocean breakers, although I have spent many days at the different beaches since then.

As I looked out over the largest body of water in the world, watching the waves follow each other in quick succession and then break upon the shore, I wondered if they would ever stop and take a rest. In my many trips to the beach, it was always the same everlasting eternal motion. Sometimes breaking close in and sometimes farther out, but with the waves always coming in and never reaching beyond a certain limit. I might have said already that it was a long way from the Plains to the Pacific Ocean, which was true regarding my many and varied experiences, but in distance it was only about halfway across our great nation.

As I thought about this almost endless body of water in contrast to the hot, dry, barren plains that I had known, I thought of how much good a little of it might do if it were turned loose on the desert (minus the salt, of course). But then, who am I that I should complain of God's arrangement of things on this old earth? For, after all, is this not God's work according to His own great plan for creation? Taking the waters from the seas and spreading them over the land, minus the salt, and leaving the inland deserts, perhaps, to man's ingenuity, giving him something to do to keep him out of so much devilment. We hear so much these days about building a new world when men have not yet learned enough to run the one that God has already given us, but are forecasting new devices to blast it to pieces and bring death and destruction upon themselves and everyone else.

In the times of which I have been writing, about 1910, the automobile was just in the experimental stage. So to get to the seaside in those days was by way of the old sternwheeler riverboats down the Columbia River to Astoria, and then sixteen miles to the ocean beach by train. The boats carried freight as well as passengers and stopped at every landing to take on and leave off freight. It was about a full day's trip one way, and the fare was one dollar, and a real dinner was served for fifty cents. There were only just a few passengers on board, and they became acquainted with each other more or less and just had a good time together. Even the captain himself became friendly. I can recall those river trips with a great deal of pleasure, and sometimes wish I could live them over again. When the boat would glide along so silently on the breast of the old Columbia and the soft, cool breeze would fan a person into a feeling of new life. But what's the use? I better get back to my story.

After two or three days at the beach, we returned to Felida, and the summer was passed in me helping Dad Cameron with his orchard work and then taking care of other chores around his place until the prune harvest began. There was plenty to do until the prune crop was all at the dryer, as Dad had a good crop of prunes that year. He and I done just about all the harvesting and hauling ourselves without any help from the outside to speak of. I made a trip to Hood River after the prunes were taken care of and took a job for a week or so picking apples so that I might learn something about the apple business. I was looking around trying to find a suitable place and a business I thought I could make a go of. But apple orchard land was so high, I gave it up and came back to Felida.

I was in a quandary to know what to do, as I could see that the children were annoying the old folks quite a bit, and I wanted to take them away. If I had not leased the Wyoming ranch, I think I would have taken them back to the hills again, but as I was "out of there" for two and a half more years, I had to do something. So when there was a ten-acre prune orchard with a small house, a dryer, and a storeroom on it, offered for five thousand dollars, I thought I would buy it. That would give us a place to live until the time when the lease would run out on the Wyoming place and then I would go back there again and sell the prune farm. But something happened to change my plans, as often happens in the course of a lifetime.

Well, I made arrangements and bought the new place, then took Pearl and Fred and just batched and tried to take care of them for a while. That did not work out so well, as I was tied up and unable to get away from the house to do any work. So then I tried to hire a woman to come and help take care of them, but for reasons I will not mention here, that arrangement did not work out so good. The next summer, a nice older couple offered to come and stay for a while, just for a place to live until they could get settled on a place of their own. That proved to be a satisfactory solution to my problem until something else came to pass, something which has always seemed to me to have been God's kind intervention in the affairs of my life.

I had become pretty badly discouraged at times, and if it had not been for the two little children and my conscience always reminding me of my obligations as a father to them, I guess I would have let loose and done the wrong thing. But something always happened to keep me trying. As for instance, one morning I was lying in bed feeling pretty blue and feeling sorry for myself when little Freddy put his little arms around my neck and put his freckled face up to mine and said, "I 'woves' you Daddy" and that acted on me like a spiritual tonic.

Although that has been over thirty-five years ago, it has never been forgotten, as it reminded me that I still had something to live for, and although he was just a very little boy, he taught me a lesson that all the wise men in the world could not have taught me. How true the Lord's words that come to me as I write this, "And a little child shall lead them." It has never been forgotten. Well, I have tried to teach Freddy many lessons since then, but I doubt, with all my years of experience to back me up, that I have ever been able to make the impression on him and his life that his little baby words made on mine.

In the meantime, my brother Aaron had come West and brought Mother (who had become an invalid) with him. Although he had written me from Portland and given me an address, when I went to look for it, there had been some mistake in the address, and I could not find Aaron's location. After writing several letters and trying to trace them up, I finally located them in Rex, Oregon. Before I could get away and visit them, Mother had died and was buried in the Newberg cemetery. So, as I said before, I had bid her goodbye for the last time in Wyoming at the Cow Creek ranch. Well, life had so ordered things that I was to see very little of my father and mother in life and was not even to be present when they were laid to rest.

Well, the opportunity came at last for me to go and visit Aaron and his family, as I had written and received several letters from him. In one of my letters, I had said something about my problems, and he had said to come over, and he might be able to show me a way to solve some of my difficulties. I guess with Aaron being an older brother, I thought he might be able to give me some good advice. As I had not seen him for several years and had never met his wife, I thought I would take a vacation and go and visit them. When I got off the train at Rex and climbed the long hill back into a wilderness of fir trees, I wondered just why he had hidden himself and his family away in a place like that, and then I remembered that he had always liked the hills. So by following a trail for some distance back through the trees, I finally came to a little clearing with a newly built board house.

When I went to the door, there was a tall young lady who met me there. I asked her if she was Mrs. Slothower, and she said, "No, I am her sister, but she will be here in a few moments." As she just thought I was another one of those pestering sales agents, I made myself known as Aaron's brother, and she at once became interested and asked, "You are Robert, aren't you?" I said yes, and she said, "I am Leonia." And although I had already heard lots about the girl through my mother and otherwise, I had never met the girl or the name before. At the time, it seemed such a strange name and hard for me to remember. But the girl just seemed to me like I had known her all my life, and she would have been mighty hard to forget. It did not take me long to fall in love with both the name and the girl, especially the girl, and it did not take long to find that our feelings toward each other were mutual.

I will stop just long enough here to say that our love for each other has never failed us through the nearly thirty-five years of trials, sickness, and deaths that have come to us. I'm sure this is true for most people who take upon themselves the responsibilities of raising a family.

Well, Leonia's sister Ruth soon came, and as Aaron was working at a little sawmill close by, I did not get to see him until evening, but I did not find it dull waiting. When my newly found friend asked me if I would like to see Aaron's garden, as she wanted to get some vegetables for dinner, I was afraid that I failed somewhat in appreciating the beauty of the garden as my eyes kept wandering back to the tall young girl who had so suddenly come into my life, and in such an unexpected way. I could not see or think of anything else, and if we pulled some carrots that day that were insufficiently matured, I was also inclined to want to rush the season along in other lines.

After we had spent a while scraping the hide off a lot of carrots no larger than a lead pencil, my new friend baked a batch of biscuits. I will say right here, she did not win my heart through my stomach as regards to those biscuits, for they were surely sinkers. I always told her later that she must have gotten the baking powder upside down by mistake.

When Aaron came home that evening, we had a good visit and talked over old times together. We had not seen each other for six or seven years, and there was a lot to talk about. I thought I would be leaving in a day or so, but as it seemed such a restful place to me, I just lingered on.

Aaron's oldest boys, Roy and Jim, were about six and eight years old at that time. They had made up their minds that their Aunt Leonia needed a couple of guardians and that they could fill the bill pretty well, so when we went out for a walk, they thought they would follow us without our permission. One day, we were walking along a footpath, single file, with the two boys bringing up the rear when the younger of the two, Jim, suddenly decided we needed protection from the front as well. He slipped by us and got around in front of us when Roy called out to him, "Hey Jim, if you want to follow, you have to stay behind." Well, it sounded so funny to us that we never have forgotten it.

I remember one night that Aaron and I talked a long time after we went to bed (as we were sleeping in the same room). I asked him what he had meant in his letter when he said he might be able to help me get rid of some of my troubles, and he said, "Go ahead the way you are, you are doing all right." Well, one day, when we were sitting on a big log together, I decided to present the old, old story to Leonia. And, of course, realizing that I was many years her senior and that I was asking her to give up her freedom and be a mother to my two motherless children, as well as my wife. I told her to not be in a hurry to give me her answer as I wanted her to realize just how serious a thing she might be getting into. Her answer was, "If I think as much of you in two months from now, as I do now, I will marry you," and at the time, that was very satisfactory to me.

What I had intended to be a short visit extended into about a week, as near as I can remember, and each day seemed to make it a little harder for me to make up my mind to leave. Each day we spent in each other's company only added to our better understanding of each other's likes and dislikes, and we were pleased to find out we were almost of the same mind regarding the more important things in life. Although our courtship was very short, I am sure we learned more about each other in that short time than most people do in a much longer courtship. We were trying to use our heads as well as our hearts, and I am sure that our mutual understanding of each other has served us well during the nearly thirty-five years of our married life.

I think that it is too often the case that young people are led into hasty marriages by human impulses and don't use the brains that God gave them to think things out. Well anyway, I am sure that the good Lord had something to do with bringing us together just at the time when we both were needing each other so badly. I can never forget, one morning when we stood together on the top of a hill overlooking a beautiful valley, with the rolling green hills as a background. There seemed to be an unknown power coming down and filling my soul with such a feeling of peace and happiness that I had never experienced before in my life. I think God was trying to show me that life was worth the living after all. Well, it all ended up with Leonia telling me to come back in a month and she would be ready to go with me, and thus it was settled. We have often heard the saying that absence makes the heart grow fonder. We only gave it a month to work on us, and it had fairly good results.

It so happened that the year I had bought the ten-acre prune orchard, I had also bought a heavy crop of prunes, and the trees were a picture to look at. The price prospect was good, and when I got home, I got things in shape as much as I could for the coming harvest. As I had gone into the woods earlier in the season and cut my own dryer wood, I hired a man to haul it out for me and done a number of other things that needed looking after. I told the old couple who had been staying with the children my secret, and they agreed to stay on until I had brought the bride home. I will not tire my readers by going into the details of the wedding, as it is sufficient to say that at the appointed time, I went and got Leonia and brought her to Vancouver. We were married there by the Christian minister on the twenty-second of August 1911, and we spent about a week on our honeymoon, most of it at the beach at Seaside. As Leonia had never seen the ocean before, we were of one mind about it and spent as much time as we could out on the beach watching the breakers roll in. Through the years that have passed since then, whenever we have had time for a vacation, we most always go somewhere to an ocean beach. And, by the way, that is my idea of a good time, just lying around in the warm sand and watching the sea.

(Paddle Wheeler T. J. on the Lower Columbia, old postcard, 1901, photographer unknown. Public domain, Wikipedia)

We came back to Portland on the old Potter, and it was so crowded that we had a hard time getting a place at the supper table. We did not enjoy the crowd very much, as we were not accustomed to crowds, and we were glad to get to a hotel where we could rest up awhile. The next day we took the train for Felida. When we got off the train there was nothing there but a little old station house, with a log-rafting outfit on one side and a big steep hill on the other. I guess Leonia must have been wondering where the nice prune orchards were. At least that is what almost everyone else who has ever come on that train has wondered, but when we got to the top of the hill, the orchards at that time spread out on both sides. They were all kept up and were a beautiful sight. As I look out over this same section of country today and see the wreck of what once was the most prosperous prune section of the northwest, it is hard to realize that I am living in the same place and looking over the same landscape.

We arrived home and found two very curious children waiting to see their new mother, and I am sure Leonia was just as curious about the rest of the family. Whatever their feelings were at the time, it does not matter so much, as it was not long before they were getting acquainted, and a feeling of contentment came over me such as I had not known for a long time. I guess something had happened to me that was far better than anything I ever expected to have happened in this world. Although Pearl and Fred had left long ago and each have two children of their own now, they both think of Leonia as the only mother they ever knew. And she loves them both just the same as if she had brought them into the world herself.

Our arrival home was seen by one of the young men of the community, and of course, we expected some visitors that night, and I had made preparations for them by buying a box of cigars and plenty of candy. When bedtime came, we just blew out the light and did not go to bed. When the noise started, Pearl stuck her little head out the window and shouted, "Go to it boys I am not afraid!" Then I opened the door and called them in, and we treated them to such as we had, and I sang and played some of the old songs for them. They went away happy, and if they did not smoke all of the cigars, it did not matter. I could finish them myself, for I was a smoker at that time.

The day we arrived home from our honeymoon trip happened to be Pearl's seventh birthday, August 27, 1911. Leonia had got her a locket for a birthday present, which pleased Pearl very much. At that time, our living quarters were rather small, as we only had a three-room shack, but Leonia made the best of it, as she has always been willing to do when things were not as convenient as we would have liked. That is one thing that has contributed greatly to a long and happy married life.

When we arrived at home, the prune crop was ripening fast, and of course, my first task was to make preparations for harvesting and drying of a crop that was new to me. I was fortunate to have gained a little experience the previous year in helping Dad Cameron with his crop and the good advice of a few good friends who had plenty of experience in the prune business. If not for this, I would have been at a loss to know just how to go about a business that was entirely different from my line of work.

But where there is a will, there is most always a way, and the first thing I knew, I was in the midst of the prune harvest. Although the old dryer was out of date and very slow, we succeeded in taking care of a very profitable crop with very little loss. And owing to the fact that good help was easy to get in those days, everything went along very satisfactorily.

Both Leonia and I were very well satisfied with the prune business, for out of less than ten acres, we were able to clear about two thousand dollars, which was better than I had been able to do with the cattle. Although that would not be considered very much these days (due to the present cost to keep a family and pay debts) we thought it was just fine back then. We even began to have visions of more orchard land and a better house to live in. I am sure that is the way with the average person as we are never willing to let well enough alone and be satisfied with things as they are. Instead, we are always willing to reach out and take on additional burdens and responsibilities for the purpose of financial gain and for getting fixed up for a more abundant life, as the saying goes.

Of course, that is just the natural spirit of progress, which has made the United States the greatest country in the world. Without it, the descendants of the pilgrim forefathers would still be milling around New England, and the country where we are now living would still be a wilderness of great fir trees, and in some ways, it might be better so. But as our forefathers were not willing to leave the prairies of the Great Plains right side up, neither were they willing to allow the great forests to stand. They cut them down and sawed them into lumber to be shipped away, not only to all parts of our own country, but to the distant markets of the world.

Not long ago, while making the trip around the Olympic Peninsula, we stopped and ate our lunch under the huge branches of a forest of towering spruce trees. Some of these would measure seven or eight feet in diameter and were of a great height, which had never been marked by axe or saw. As I looked at them, I thought that this is what our farm once looked like, aside from the smooth highway that we were traveling on. I wondered how long it would be before this too would be gone to feed the mills of progress and satisfy man's greed for gain. Then I thought of the poem "Only God Can Make a Tree." I think it would be a great thing, in some places, if men would give God a chance to make some more trees in some of those places where men have gone through and left nothing but wreck and ruin.

It has now been some time since I have written on this story. As I had gotten off the story and onto a side trip writing about trees, I might as well tell of some more trees (or parts of trees) that we saw that left an impression on me. Recently, we went to Grand Coulee Dam to visit our son Fred and his family. I will tell something of this trip now while it is still fresh in my memory, as I am inclined to forget things of late. These trees that we saw were dead trees, dead and buried away in the earth for so many thousands of years that they have turned to stone and are now, as we call them, petrified. We saw the ends of many logs that men had uncovered on the side of a hill that was barren of a single living tree. The strangest of it all, these trees were of many different varieties, some that are not known to grow in this part of the country in this age. This goes to prove that even the climate has changed since these trees grew there. Well, this is a strange world indeed, and there is good evidence stored away in the hills and rocks that this old Mother Earth has been here a long time and has undergone a good many changes that are difficult for mortal man to understand.

I have been telling of some of the works of God and nature, and now I will tell something of the greatest piece of work that man, who is the climax of all of God's creation, has done. It was our privilege on this same trip of the latter part of May 1946 to see the Grand Coulee Dam. It is said to be the greatest piece of concrete work in the world up to the present time. Thanks to the many and to our son

Fred, who has contributed five or six years of his life toward building it. He got a permit to take us not only over the dam but down inside of it, and I think we saw about all that was to be seen there.

As I looked at those great generators humming away there, turned by this great man-made waterfall, I thought what a wonderful world we would have if these great power plants would be used only for the good of mankind and the glory of God, and not for building machines for the purpose of destruction. After all, God supplied the material from which it was built, the building site upon which it stands and the water that turns the wheels. He endowed men with the power and wisdom to do the work and take from His great storehouse the things necessary and to apply the results to the benefit of mankind.

Therefore, we should see God's handiwork in it all, and we should never fail to give Him the glory. At the present time, I can sit here in my home, nearly four hundred miles from this power plant and write these pages by the light that is generated up there. The power pumps the water we use and runs the washing machine and the vacuum cleaner, it heats the electric iron, the electric plate, and the electric pad when we get a sore back, it keeps the food from spoiling in the refrigerator and so on. Why should we not thank

God? The world has come a long ways since the days of the old dugout down in Kansas.

Well, I think I have been on the side track long enough, so I better get back on the main line again. I now continue my story from the fall of 1911. I had just harvested my first prune crop, and I was feeling pretty good about having such a successful year. Not only did we have a good crop, but I had also gained a wonderful wife to share my joys and sorrows. I do not recall anything of much importance happening during the winter of 1911/1912, only than that I was trying to learn how to prune the trees and getting accustomed to my new line of business.

In the spring of 1912, we took on a new obligation and bought the ten acres along the east side of our place at a very high price. It had a good house and was just what I thought we needed to make us a good layout. So I sold the Wyoming ranch, and I applied the money on the new place but had to take out a mortgage for the balance due. As I have learned to my sorrow, a mortgage is an ever present sort of thing, and it never stops eating, and I have spent a good portion of my life under this particular sort of handicap.

Well, as it happened, the crop was not good that year. I remember how Leonia and I, when we started looking for our second prune crop, were very much discouraged. I think she cried a little, and I felt like it, but it finally showed up better than we had expected, and there turned out to be perhaps about half a crop there. But on the tenth of August, 1912, something else happened that proved to be a full crop with two extra or three crops in one, for that was the day the triplets were born.

Were we all kept busy for a while, standing guard night and day, the clothesline never empty, and the concert of voices was a common thing. We turned the kitchen into a nursery and baby Charles was so small, at first, he fit into a shoebox. So it was that Leonia became the mother of a large family in a short time, and as this happened just before prune drying time, I knew we needed some ready cash. I had never borrowed from the bank here and was a little apprehensive that perhaps I might be turned down, but when the banker asked me if I was the father of those triplets, and I said, "I guess I am guilty," he said that a man who is the father of triplets should have anything he asks for. He let me have three hundred dollars, and we kept the triplets.

I do not think I shall go into much detail regarding the few years that followed the birth of the triplets as there was nothing out of the ordinary that happened then. It is sufficient to say that it was all we could do to keep the little fellows alive for a while. Leonia was in poor health, and it was hard to get the help she needed. Somehow, through God's kind providence, they lived and grew up into two fine young men. The third triplet was a wonderful girl who died at almost twenty-three years old, leaving a husband and two little girls who are now almost grown into young womanhood.

The readers of this story will notice I have mentioned God many times in the course of this narrative. This is not because I knew Him so very well back when the different acts of this story took place, but rather because I have learned to know Him better at the time in which I am writing. As a believer in a personal Savior, I can now look back over the years and recognize when God interceded in the affairs of my life many times, though I did not recognize His kind providence at the time. This story would not be complete if I did not tell of what (to me) was the most important event in the course of my whole life. Important because it changed my whole outlook on life here on earth and gave me the hope of a world to come. I will now tell how it happened.

There was a woman holding revival meetings here at the church, and a lot of pressure was brought to bear on me to go and hear her preach, but I was like most everyone else, ready to make excuses of all kinds. I guess I thought religion was all right for anyone else but me. So I just put it off until one evening Leonia won her point and got me to go to church with her. As I sat there and listened, I recognized that this woman believed the Bible and was preaching it as the word of God. She believed in Jesus Christ as the Savior of mankind and of lost sinners in particular. It was not long before I got under conviction, and when she asked me if I was a Christian, I said yes, I was trying to be, but she knew I was lying by my guilty looks. She said nothing more to me at the time, but I am sure she did some praying for this old sinner, for I got under conviction so badly that I could not sleep at night.

When Leonia asked me again to go to church with her, I said, "If I go up there, I will have to go forward." She said, "Suppose you do, that won't hurt you." So I finally gave in and went with her, and then was when it happened. Both she and I went up together, and it seemed that all the sins of a lifetime were crushing me down, and I should hide my face in shame. As I was kneeling there at the altar with my face hidden, Mrs. "S" said, "Look up Brother, you will never find him down there." As I raised my face and looked up, this was my prayer: "Oh God, give me a clean heart." Just seven words, and it was done. I can never explain the wonder of it, as I rose from my knees and turned and looked the people in the face, and the shame I had felt was all gone. Instead of that terrible conviction, a great peace had come into my heart, such as I had never known before. A new courage came with it, and I could walk back into the congregation and try to get someone else saved. I was a new creature, born again, just as Jesus told Nicodemus, "Ye must be born again."

Well, I went home, and when I opened the Bible, God opened it also, and I saw the truth through the eyes of the spirit of God and understood it. And to anyone who cannot understand the Bible, I will say, ask God to open your eyes, for the eyes of sinful flesh cannot see and understand it. You will never understand all of it in this life, but God will show you all you need to know, and as a mother increases the portion of a child's feed as it is able to digest it, so does the Lord increase our understanding of His Word, as we need it.

It was a happy time for Leonia and me when, with mutual consent, we sought the Lord together, and in all that time of over thirty years, He has not failed us in time of need. He has helped us over many a dark valley, and when death came to our family, He did not dispel the angel of death but gave us sufficient of His wonderful grace to carry us through and give us peace. We can never understand why God allows these hard things to come to us as Christians, but He has said, "It will rain on the unjust as well as the just," and this rule of God's dealings with people holds good in most all of His dealings with both Christians and non-Christians. I suppose if God should show His followers too many material blessings, the world would seek Him for the loaves and fishes or the material blessings and benefits, and not for the unselfish devotion to the cause for which He came into this world.

I do not know if this story will reach anyone outside the circle of our family or whether it will even be read by all of them, but I have had the satisfaction of telling this old story of salvation through faith in Jesus Christ as the very Son of God and my personal Savior. It helps me even now, as I write these words on this blank piece of paper which cannot see or hear or speak, except when I or someone else places the words down here to speak for us. When a person becomes a Christian, they are subject to a certain amount of criticism by the world in general. This is because it is not possible for an unbeliever to understand these things, for they are spiritually understood, as I said about the Bible. But I have noticed that most of the criticism comes from those who do not know any better and are willing to show it by arguing against something they know nothing about. I will venture to say that if anyone is anxious to know the truth and will honestly seek it, God will show it to him. I am just throwing in this extra comment because I would not miss this opportunity to point my readers toward "The Lamb of God Who taketh away the sin of the world," as John the Baptist did when he pointed to Christ (see John 1:29).

If you are already a Christian and have already found the way, you will be happy to know that this writer is a believer and on the divine path. And we can rejoice together someday in that wonderful home that He has gone to prepare for those who love Him. The cowboy sings of his home on the range. Well, I have spent many days on the open range and can testify to the free and easy feeling that comes over a person when he is riding a good horse out there on the open range. But I also can testify to the fact that it is not all free and easy, for I have put in some of the hardest days of my life out there in the heat and dust and dirt and sweat, wrestling cattle and branding calves.

I have often come in at night so tired I could hardly walk and so dirty that a glimpse back into my old hobo days would have made me look like a gentleman in comparison. This is the side of the "Home on the Range" that the poets do not sing about. And it is my honest conviction that most of the cowboy poets have never experienced this other side of the "Home on the Range." I have written a poem that can be sung to the old tune of "Home on the Range." That is my earnest prayer for everyone. And were it fulfilled, we would all have not only a much happier home on this earth, but also a more definite hope of a happier home in the world to come. So I think I shall give the words of the song here, as it seems an appropriate place for it. To those who know their Bibles, I will say that you will be able to find many Bible references that these words are based on. They are altogether my own words, but I hope they conform to God's will and purpose, for they were inspired by a dream I had.

An Old Ranger's Prayer for 1945

Lord, give us the light that shines through the night
Of the darkness that troubles our days
By faith let us see a world that is free
And filled with thy love and thy praise
By faith let us look for that city foursquare
Coming down from the Father above
Lord, help us to pray and hasten the day
When the world will be filled with Thy love.
Chorus: Home, home over there
In the place Thou hast gone to prepare
Where there is no night and Christ is the light
And His glory forever we'll share.
Lord, give us the bread that we might be fed
On the manna that came from on high
And give us to drink of the water of life
From the well that will never run dry
O, help us to look for His coming again
With the power to set this world free
When the knowledge of God shall cover the earth
As the water that covers the sea.
(chorus)

And so now, as God has been kind enough to let me live beyond my three score and ten years of my allotted time, according to the Bible, I find a great deal of pleasure in looking back over the past and trying to bring these things out of the secret archives of my memory. As I write them down here for others to see and read (if they will), I myself get a great measure of satisfaction in living them over again, although some of those happenings were not so pleasant.

As I realize that I am nearing the time when I shall take my leave of this "House of Clay," which has caused me and others quite a bit of annoyance at times, I can look forward as well as backward. And by faith, I can see a very much happier life and a far better world than the one we live in today. And I am trusting that a just Judge Who never makes the wrong decision will see something of sufficient value in the good that I have tried to do, that it might outweigh the mistakes sufficiently that He will let me pass. I can say with Paul that I know that if our earthly house made of this tabernacle were dissolved, "We have a building of God, a house not made with hands, eternal in the heavens." (2 Corinthians 5:1)

Such was my conversion, and such is my faith in a Savior Who has cared for us all these years. Why should we not trust Him to take care of the future?

There has never been a trying problem that came our way, either of our lives or our children's, that has not been taken to Him in prayer. And each time He has seen us through in a wonderful way, although not always to our liking. God's way is the best way, but sometimes, it takes a long time to find it out. And so, my dear children, I close this account of my conversion. Please do not pass it up too lightly or think of it as an overwrought condition of my mind caused by thinking too much along this line of thought. Rather, think of it as a change of heart brought about by having faith that the Lord would do just what He promised to do. All through the years, from the time when you were just little children, when we took you with us to Sunday school and church, sometimes, perhaps, when you did not want to go. It was with the earnest desire that you would be kept by His loving care and that you would not become subject to making the mistakes in life that most people seem to make. We have tried not to discourage you by overdoing it or by being too strict, as it were, allowing you the freedom to make your own decisions when you grew older and praying to God always for your eternal welfare. We are leaving you in His hands, and may He watch over and keep you always. That is my prayer.

This might be a very good conclusion to my story, but owing to the fact that it is thirty-four years this summer since the birth of the triplets, my readers would wonder if there was nothing of sufficient interest that took place in all that time to find a place for it in my story. Something besides my conversion of which I have just told about. To which I will say that there were many interesting events that happened during that period of nearly half of my lifetime. But this story has grown to greater length than I ever dreamed of when I started to write it, and therefore, I will consider only a few of the more important events. To those who would like a more detailed account, I will refer them to my diaries, which I started to keep on March 1, 1918. I have kept up pretty faithfully until the present time with the exception of one book that was lost, and a few times when I was too busy and tired out to keep up-to-date with my records. Anyway, I think my children will have a pretty good idea of what kind of a time their dad had in getting through this world up to the present time if they will read all I have left to read.

Of course, there was not much change in everyday life on the prune farm for many years, just ups and downs, as the saying goes. One year would be a good year, and the next we would go into the red. But taking it as a whole, we managed to live, pay interest and taxes, and send the five children to school and finally through high school, which was the best we could do for them. At first, we used horses to do the farming with, and then I got the tractor working, at first just in my head, and was not satisfied until I had it working in the orchard (and also on my bank account to pay for repairs). Remember back then in 1918, the tractor was still more or less in the experimental stage. Many times I had tractor parts scattered all over the yard, but I would finally get them all assembled again and on the move. A part of my equipment was a device of my own making, a combination clod masher, harrow and leveler that could raise more dust than a Kansas cyclone, if possible. The triplets' favorite pastime was to get on the thing and ride it. And in my imagination, I can see them yet as the dust would clear away for a moment and reveal their black faces and shining eyes, but it was only dirt and would all come off in the bathtub.

Friday, October 17, 1947

It has now been well over a year since I have written on my story, and I have often wondered if I should ever write anymore. Here I sit alone today in the old Felida home and listen to the wind howling around the eves of the house. I watch the beautiful fir tree through the window as the wind stirs its branches. I think about how it has grown to such proportions since the happenings I have related now going back twenty-five years ago. I got to thinking of the changes that have come to pass in that period of time, not only in the tree, but in the country around us. Also, of the destiny of our family, who have grown up and have gone to different places and have families of their own. It made me feel rather lonely, and I just wanted to talk to somebody, and as there was no one else present, I just felt inclined to put my thoughts down here where someone might read them sometime. Since I last wrote, several things have happened that I will mention.

I had wished to finish the story in a house of our own by the Pacific Ocean, where I could sit in a comfortable place and look out over the vast expanse of the largest body of water on earth. And watch the breakers as they roll in, sometimes low and rather smooth, other times rough and high. Then I could say, "This is the last frontier for me" in a place that would make the title of my story come true, *From the Plains to the Pacific*. But so far, our home by the sea is only a cabin of just twelve by twenty-two feet, and we only visit it occasionally. Perhaps we may yet realize our dream, but if not, we still thank God for this wonderful home here. Especially, for the pleasant memories it brings to us when we think back over the years and live again in memory of some of our pleasant experiences with family and friends. Some of them have gone beyond the last frontier and have left vacancies that can never be filled, as it seems, this side of heaven. We hope and pray we may meet them again in a place where there will be no parting.

The prune orchards that once surrounded us are nearly all gone, and our part of the country has undergone great change, in both the kind of crops raised and in the people who live here. It seems the house of God is almost deserted now. Mother is away today trying to do something to help revive the old church, but there is little cooperation at the present time to do this. Perhaps in time and with God's help, the things hoped and prayed for may come to pass again. Perhaps when the old church trees have all been dug up and rooted out, a new crop may be grown in the same old soil and will produce abundantly for the Lord. But it cannot be done by planting any other seed than the word of God.

Sometimes I have trouble continuing with my story, but if the opportunity affords and the urge to write comes, I would like to put the finish to it with my pen and not quit before I have said all that should be said. Before I write the finish, I would like to pay a fitting tribute to each member of my family, beginning with the mothers and coming on down the line to the youngest.

Leonia and Robert at home, Felida, WA, mid 1920's

Afterthoughts

I was just reading in *Reader's Digest* about the large redwood trees of California with their towering height of three hundred feet or more, and it reminded me of another tree that was a sheltering refuge of mine on the old herd ground in Kansas. This tree from my earlier days was very much in contrast to those towering giants of California. This old elm tree stood on the banks of Skunk Creek, about one half mile north of our old stone house, and it was all alone as there was not another thing that could be called a tree in nearly a half-mile radius.

This tree was a large tree as trees go in that part of Kansas, but it was very low to the ground, with wide-spreading branches just high enough so that I could jump up and grab hold of them and pull myself up into them. The limbs were very thick, with dense foliage that made it not only a shelter from the hot sun but from the storms as well, many times I found protection from the falling hailstones there. It was very old and twisted, and the roots were exposed for some distance going out from the tree, owing to the tramping feet of animals that had found shelter there, perhaps for hundreds of years. I expect many a buffalo fought each other for a place under its protective branches long before white men ever invaded the West. Such is the picture of my old elm tree, and I expect it is still there, unless it has died of old age because no one would ever try to make wood out of an old tough elm tree such as that one. It is a hard task to split the best of them.

Well, one of my cattle herd was an old, gentle milk cow we called Pet, and I could milk her anywhere on the range. Sometimes, the lunch they gave me did not suit my fancy, and I would give it to old Pet and then milk her into either a cup or my mouth. As it was an even exchange, she never kicked about it. If I heard any discussions at home about "Old Pet" not giving any milk at night, I never let on that I knew anything about it, and as "Old Pet" kept the secret too, I guess they never knew the real cause of it.

One hot summer day, the cattle had hunted the shade and were lying around panting and trying to keep cool. As there was no immediate danger of their invading the cornfield, I also lay down in the shade of the old elm and went to sleep. I was suddenly awakened by something crushing my hand and woke to see it all skinned up and bleeding where Pet had stepped on it. She had come around looking for more lunch, and I guess that was her way of waking me up. Of course, I had a very sore hand for a while.

There were the wild plum patches grouped around here and there, with a variety of size, shape, and flavor of plums. Some red, some purple, and some yellow, all with a different flavor. There were also many different varieties of wild grapes, some large and some small, some fairly sweet, but most sour enough to make a pig squeal. Some would spread along the ground and some would climb the trees to the very top, hanging there until wintertime, and the grapes would dry on the vine. We thought they were good to eat, even at that stage, but we kids would eat anything and think it was good, even the sumac berries, which were even worse than the wild grapes.

Then we would take the stalks of the sumac bush, punch the pith out of it, and make popguns to shoot paper wads. We used the willows to make whistles that would vary in tone according to their size and the amount of air pressure we would put on them. I must not forget the sugarcane that used to grow so high with its silky black heads waving in the breeze. And the sorghum mill with its long sweep and bright shining steel rolls with the horse going round and round. The sorghum juice ran out of a long spout and into copper kettles, where it was cooked until it was considered thick enough and black enough to be called molasses or blackstrap. I fed many a dose of it to old Pet when it was spread on my lunch, and I suppose she lived to be of mature age.

Not long after I went to live at the "S" home, I somehow got possession of a cheap mouth harp. Like most kids, I supposed that they were just something to make a noise with, as I had never heard anyone play a tune on one of them. After tooting away on it for some time, I discovered that by using my tongue and getting my mouth in the right shape, I could get a few notes out of it that sounded a little like the starting of a tune. After a while, I was able to play *Nelly Gray* well enough that Mr. "S", when he heard me one evening, stood still and listened in wonder at anyone being able to get a tune out of a thing like that. To my great surprise and pleasure, one day when he came back from town, he had bought me a new, original Comet Schalltrichter mouth harp and had paid thirty-five cents for it. Well, it was not long before I could play it, and every Christmas as long as I stayed with them, he never failed to get me one of those same make of mouth harp, considered the best there was at that time, and soon after that, there were a number of mouth harp players around there.

When herding cattle, I almost always carried a stick around with me that I used for killing snakes or any other use I might have for it, and I killed quite a number of rattlesnakes. I remember one close call I had with a very large rattler, only on this day, I did not have my club. I guess, like all boys and dogs, I liked to hunt rabbits, and the day I am telling about, I had spotted a cottontail rabbit and took after him. He ran into some thick bunch grass and I thought he had dodged down into a hole in the ground, so I ran up quickly to try to catch him.

When I threw myself onto my hands and knees to look down into the hole, right there within a few inches of my face was a very large rattler, all coiled up and ready to strike. I jerked myself back and was on my feet like a flash, but the snake had struck at the same time and was now lying full length at my feet, getting ready for a new assault. I made my escape, went and got a stick, and came back and found him, and I done the next striking myself.

That was a close shave for me. I removed the rattles, and I think there were twelve or thirteen of them. Since the stick I had used was pretty light, I was not sure I had done a good job of killing him, so the next day, I took my real club and looked for him again. It was a long time before I found him, as he had crawled away in the thick grass. When I did find him he was all coiled up and seemed to be well on the way to recovery, minus the rattles. Well, I did a short job of finishing him off, and the next day I saw a buzzard flying away with the remains.

One evening, just before I started the cattle for home, I looked up and saw a strange critter coming full speed into the herd. It proved to be a steer, about a year and a half old, and although he was a very nice-looking steer, he looked rather wild about the eyes, and I did not wish to have him in the bunch. As this was before Rover's time, I tried to run him off, but he seemed to like his new associates and would not leave them, so I let him get in with the herd. Mr. "S" advertised him, trying to find the owners. Of course, I thought I might get the reward, but as it went on for several weeks and no one claimed him, I began to think maybe he might belong to me someday.

One day, Mr. S's oldest boy, the one I had pulled out of the river, came along, and this steer seemed to take a dislike to him and started for him. Before I could get ahead of him, he had Albert down and pinned to the ground, and Albert was yelling like sixty by the time I got there with my club and ran him off (I mean the steer).

After that, Mr. "S" was anxious to get rid of him while I was still looking for my reward. Then one evening, after the steer had stayed with us a month or so, he suddenly decided that his visit had run out, and he headed off in the direction from which he had come. Though I ran after him for about a mile and a half, I could not turn him back, and that is the last we ever heard of him. Well, people sometimes go off their base and do strange things, but that is one of the very few times I ever saw a four-legged critter do anything crazy, except for the mad dogs that came through that country a few times and had the people almost scared to death.

There was one family who had a pet dog that went mad. He had bitten the whole family—father, mother, and all three children—before they knew he was mad. There was an old Indian doctor around at the time, and he said he knew a party who had a remedy that would help them. So they sent for it and used it on the family, and it seemed to work on all of them but the man. He took down with a case of pneumonia but seemed at first to be recovering from it. Then he suddenly went mad, and although he was a small man, it took three men to hold him down when the spells came on. They asked me one time to go with two other men to stay overnight with him, and though I did not like it very much, I went just the same. By this time, he was too far gone to have a violent spell and he just laid there and frothed at the mouth and looked terrible. I shall never forget that experience. I think I was about sixteen at the time. The man died that morning.

I should tell about planting corn with the Lister, a type of plow with a moldboard on each side, which would throw the ground both ways and leave a deep, wide furrow. It had a combined drill that ran behind it in the bottom of the furrow, which planted the corn down below the bottom of the furrow and placed one grain at a time at a spacing of about a foot and a half apart. The idea was to plant the corn deep so that it could withstand the dry weather. Well, this was a very heavy rig, and we hitched four big horses to it abreast. When a field was planted, it looked like just a succession of ditches, about four feet apart. When I was fifteen or sixteen, it was my job to run that outfit and keep that four-horse team straight, taking special care to keep them from getting tangled up while turning at the ends of the field.

One of the team was a big black Percheron stallion and one was a mare, and he was always trying to make love to her, which did not help matters any. Well, after the corn was up a few inches, we had to work the soil back into the furrows, pushing it in around the corn, but taking care not to cover it up. In doing this, we had to break the horses to walk on top of the ridges, which was contrary to their usual training, as they are broke to walk in the bottom, and that was some job. When the corn furrow was successfully laid in this way, the ground would be heaped up around the plants, and the roots would be down deep. When the dry weather came, you could generally count on a good crop, while corn planted with the regular planter often failed.

Some will wonder, perhaps, if I ever saw a wild buffalo. One time, when I was very small and we were traveling along the road with a wagon, we came to the top of a ridge, and I looked over the other side. There I saw a long line of brown animals with shaggy-looking heads and necks and big shoulders, trailing along in the direction of what looked like a river. I think I heard that Dad killed one of them for meat. I am sure it was a band of buffalo on their way to water. I can remember the trails they made in the earth by constantly going back and forth on their way to and from their watering places. These trails were still in evidence long after the buffalo were gone, and so were the buffalo wallows, where they evidently stood around fighting flies and pawing the earth. These places were still there when I left Kansas, and in a heavy rain, they would fill with water and make good breeding places for mosquitoes, which were plentiful in Kansas.

Other evidence of the buffalo (and of the everlasting greed of man) could be seen everywhere in the white-bleached and shining skulls and bones of the animals lying in piles where men had shot them down. Very often, hunters just took their hides (so they said), leaving their carcasses to rot where they fell or be consumed by the coyotes. Sometimes there would only be a skull laying on the ground. I suppose this was when the settlers needed the meat, which was alright.

Well, my first recollection of Kansas is those piles of bones bleaching in the sun, but man found a way to make money even out of those old bones when the bone hunter commenced to come. They would gather them up, haul them away, and then ship them somewhere to be either ground into fertilizer or used for other purposes. When Mr. "S" heard of this chance to make a few dollars out of bones, he got busy, and we gathered up a whole mountain of them. I guess he thought he was going to get a corner on the bones market, for they stayed there in that big pile for a long time, but finally a fellow came along who bought them and took them away to the railroad. And so this is how the Kansas plains were cleared of bones and the evidence of man's inhumanity to animals.

I should say a word here about the buffalo grass, which almost completely covered the ground, except for the bottomland, and was as thick as the wool on a sheep's back. It was no doubt the natural feed for the buffalo, and it was also a godsend to the early settlers, providing pasture grass for their stock, summer and winter. There are places where, if things had been left right side up, there would not have been so many dust storms. For thousands of acres of good pastureland would have remained on lands that became, at least for a time, nothing but a barren wasteland.

A word here about the old prairie breaker called the "grasshopper," which had so much to do with turning this sod over in the first place. It was constructed with a long beam, very close to the ground, and had a shaft that was almost straight across, with rods instead of moldboards to turn the sod with. It used either a standard or rolling cutter and had a gauge wheel to regulate the depth. Of course, it had the usual handles that are fitted to any walking plow, and it would turn usually about a sixteen-inch furrow. With about three good horses, it was an inspiration to see that prairie sod get turned upside down in a slow easy turn that would never leave a break in the furrow or scarcely a spear of grass in sight. This sod was the material that many of the early settler's houses were built from, by cutting it up in lengths with a spade in sizes that a man could handle. And I have seen fairly good corn raised by planting it in this prairie sod with a sod planter without a bit of cultivation. I wish I had one of those "old time" sweet, juicy watermelons right now that were grown in the same way.

I shall tell about the prairie chickens that had their home out on a high ridge, about a mile from where I lived for so many years. In the early morning, they made the most peculiar mumbling sound, which could be heard very plainly for a long distance, and they were so plainly seen in the morning when the sun was shining. They looked so big when they ruffled their feathers and strutted around like a turkey gobbler. They were still there in the same old breeding ground when I left Kansas, as no one ever seemed to bother them. To the best of my knowledge, I never ate a piece of one or saw one of them very close up. It just seemed that the people did not bother them. Over on another ridge in the same quarter section was a prairie dog town where a certain species of owls lived in the same holes with the prairie dogs, another queer prank of animal and bird nature.

Postscript and Robert's Poem

Dear Reader:

Here at the end of great-grandfather Robert's story, I'm guessing that you noticed that he left you hanging a little bit. I would suggest that you treat the last few pages right before the "Afterthoughts" section as his conclusion. Just a reminder: my approach in "polishing up" Robert's story has been to keep it as true as possible to the original manuscript. With this consideration in mind, I believe that Robert (due to age) probably just "ran out of steam" and wasn't able to finish his story, but at the same time, what exists of his story is nothing short of amazing. Remember, he never even made it to the sixth grade. I have a strong hunch that he would have said much more about his immediate family members, as he intended to do, if he would have had a little more time and energy.

In further reflection, I did note two important omissions in Robert's story. First, Robert never mentions being abandoned by their mother. How it must have felt for him and the other two children left behind on the homestead in Kansas. This was when their mother had left for Denver with their little sister Cora and she never returned. One cousin told me that Robert's parents were estranged for a while during this time. Perhaps this was Robert's way, better to not mention it than to criticize one of his parents.

The second curious omission is related to his relatives service during the Civil War, especially the death of his Grandfather Chapman in the notorious Andersonville Prison in Georgia. Robert does mention that his father was a war veteran in the Denver chapter. Robert's father, father-in-law, one grandfather, and three of his uncles all served in the Union Army during the Civil War. I believe this was an important element in the creation of Robert's character, although unspoken by Robert in the manuscript. I've included some supplementary information in the last chapter on their contribution.

I don't believe Robert intentionally left out the accomplishments of his oldest child so I will share a couple of them with you here. Of course, I'm talking about my grandmother, Pearl Slothower Harman. As mentioned in the Wyoming chapter, Pearl was born on the Cameron homestead near Marshall, Wyoming in 1904. Pearl was six years old when Robert moved the family to Southwest Washington State.

In the mid 1920's Pearl accepted a position to teach in a one-room school house on the Hoh River in a remote rain forest region on the Olympic Peninsula in Washington. This is where my grandfather met her. Pearl was a pioneer in her own right and I believe she always carried her father's spirit with her, and I'm sure Robert was proud of her. I think she passed some of that spirit on to me. She was a great teacher for many years, and the most wonderful grandmother someone could ever have.

In conclusion, I'm just so thankful for what Robert left us; what a gift and what an inspiration! Such an amazing life Robert had, spanning eighty-one years. And there may be more to come. Just last year one of my cousins gave me two of Robert's old photo albums and the journals he started in 1918. My desire (and Robert's) is simply that this book be shared with those who might be interested.

Robert was a man who loved God, family, music, and nature. In fact, Robert refers to Joyce Kilmer's poem "Trees" in the last section, so I've shared it with you after "Robert's Poem." Joyce Kilmer, like Robert, was a family man. Sadly, Kilmer died at the age of thirty-one in WWI.

Eliza Chapman Slothower (Robert's mother) pictured above. Photo taken in Denver, CO circa 1895.

ROBERT J. SLOTHOWER AND JAMES R. HARMAN

Robert's Poem

Son and grandson of Civil War heroes,
From Pennsylvania they came.
Sod house, prairie grass and drought,
Robert almost lost his name.

A boy apart from his kin,
On the plains for seven years.
His pony and the thunderclouds,
Were better than his lonely tears.

Spring of '92, Wyoming called his name,
Went to join his brothers, from Denver they came.
To the little cabin on Cow Creek, to work and start anew.
The land was tough and unforgiving,
But not without music and antelope stew.

There's something about the hills around Garrett,
The ranchers know it to this day.
As Laramie Peak's doorstep,
They know why they came here to stay.

Robert met Dollie, his wife to be,
On the "Red Desert Ranch" above.
Found that old "heart to heart" connection,
And soon they fell in love.

PLAINS TO THE PACIFIC

Got married in Marshall the winter of '02,
Guests braved the bitter cold.
Then together bound,
They left to tame the land on Cow Creek,
Their dreams,…big and bold.

Lost their first two babes on the land they loved,
They rest under the sagebrush still.
They didn't give up, and three more came their way,
Pursuant of God's good will.

Then came a winter blizzard in December of '09,
Dollie had a terrible pain and there wasn't much time.
Through driving wind and snow, the
younger brother would ride.
With doctor returned the next day,
But it was too late, God had taken Dollie inside.

Their tried-and-true ranch neighbors
Did all they could to lend a hand,
But in time, Robert alone, would leave the sacred land.
Leave the land to find a new life, and a new wife,
To far-off Felida he would go.
In the land of good earth, tall trees,
And a mighty river would flow.

Quiet, tall, and strong,
Robert was a man who never gave up,
And clearly knew right from wrong.
God, family, and true friends were his guiding light,
His rock, his path to good fortune you know.
When facing tough days or for inspiration,
I sometimes reach out to him,
From my humble place here below.

by James R. Harman (great-grandson), 10/14/2017

Trees

I think that I shall never see
A poem lovely as a tree.
A tree whose hungry mouth is prest
Against the earth's sweet-flowing breast.
A tree that looks at God all day,
And lifts her leafy arms to pray;
A tree that may in Summer wear
A nest of robins in her hair.
Upon whose bosom snow has lain;
Who intimately lives with rain.
Poems are made by fools like me,
But only God can make a tree.

(Source: Poetry Magazine, Aug. 1913, poetryfoundation.org)

Historical Connections

Kansas Grasshopper Plague of 1874

(Kansapedia / Kansas Historical Society / author not provided)

I came across an interesting article and the above sketch while researching my Slothower family history. Robert talks about a similar event in his "life story" manuscript. Even though Robert was very young at the time, he did talk about how hot and dry it got on the prairie during the summer months in Kansas, and he also described the "Grasshopper Invasion" and the devastation that followed it. Of course, his father, Lewis, and his older brother Aaron were probably very much on the front lines in trying to fight off the grasshoppers to try and save the crops. This was a major event in Kansas at the time and a tremendous challenge for the pioneer families trying to raise crops on the prairie land.

(The above photo shows a typical threshing crew of Robert's time in Northern Kansas. Photo courtesy of Nebraska Historical Society RG2608-3129 by Solomon D. Butcher 1887)

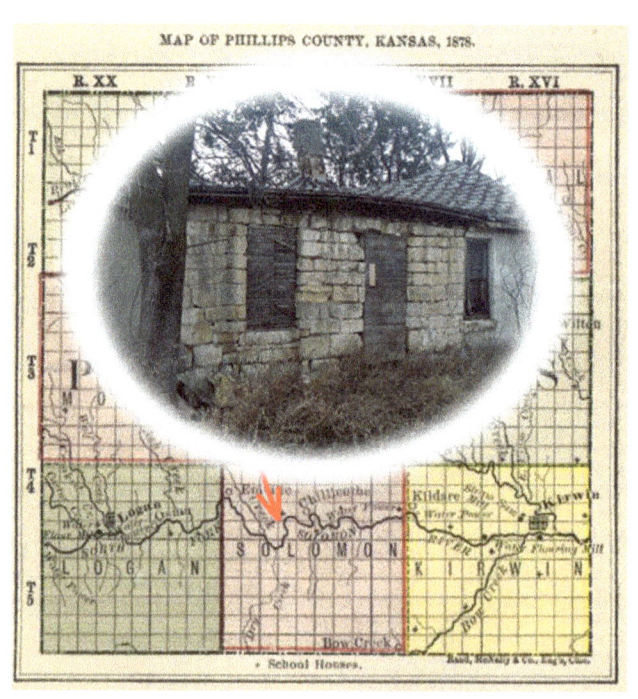

(Above insert photo courtesy of Rex Van Der Wege taken in 2018. Map of Phillips County Kansas, 1878, Rand McNally)

In the Kansas chapter, Robert talks about his father (Lewis Slothower) completing construction of their stone house about a year or so before the family gave up the homestead. Lewis started building the stone house circa 1877 and worked on it for a few years while trying to farm his homestead and do construction work for others. In the end, drought, grasshoppers, and hailstorms were too much for them and the family (like many back then) had to give up the homestead.

The insert photo on the previous page is of that same house (with roof collapsed) and was taken in September of 2018. The colored map is of Phillips County, Kansas in 1878 (Rand McNally & Co.) Mr. Van Der Wege is the present owner of what was once the Lewis Slothower homestead. Rex told me that his family had lived in the old stone house from 1948 to 1967. Several years after they had moved out of the stone house, the roof caved in, but to date, the walls are still standing. It's rather astonishing to discover that something your ancestor built 140 years ago is still standing!

The first time I made contact with Rex was in December of 2018, and he has been a wonderful resource and is familiar with several of the landmarks Robert talks about in the book. Rex's ancestors (the Winkleblecks) homesteaded a short distance north of the Slothowers and were there during the same time period. No doubt, the two families knew one another.

The Slothower stone house was somewhat of a "show place" back in the early days and for some decades to follow. Rex's great-grandmother was married there.

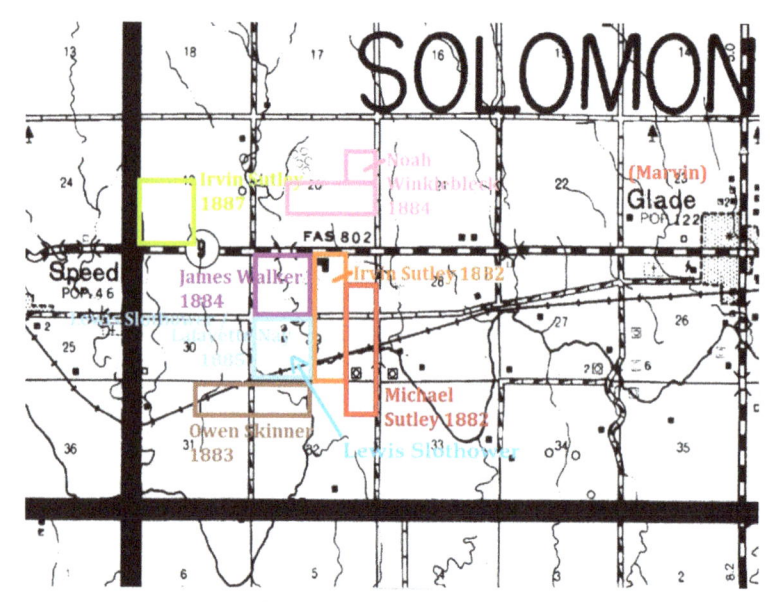

(Kansas Department. of Transportation, 1980 map of Phillips County)

Above is a map showing the location of the Lewis Slothower/ Lafayette Nay homestead in Solomon Township, Phillips County, Kansas. Skunk Creek and the small town of Marvin (now called Glade) are also shown.

Pictured to the left is Lafayette Nay, the man who took over the Lewis Slothower homestead in about 1881. Nay is also the founder of the frontier town of Marvin, Kansas, platted in 1879.
(Photo source: "Marvin Memories" page 93, Phillipsburg City Library. Taken about 1900)

Photo of Marvin Hall and members of the Cronk family, circa 1888, photographer unknown, courtesy of Steve Richardson. Celebrating Marvin, Kansas, at One Hundred Years publication, Phillipsburg Library Genealogy Room.

Robert mentions Marvin near the end of the Kansas chapter. Marvin was the closest frontier town located about four miles east of the Lewis Slothower homestead. This is where Robert and his brother Elmer met their sister Edith shortly before heading for Phillipsburg to board the train for Denver. No doubt, Robert had been to Marvin previous times as well.

Robert wrote about visiting Grand Lake, Colorado when he was in his late teens. This was during the time he lived in Denver with his family. Photo courtesy of "Visit Grand, Colorado" tourism publication)

Denver City Hall Wars

(The two previous photos were sourced from the Denver Public Library, Western Collection. They were taken in March of 1894.)

In March of 1894, Colorado Governor Wait called out the state militia to deal with some corrupt officials who had taken over the city hall building. Robert was there to witness this event and talked about it in the "Reunited in Denver" chapter. Look closely, and you can see some of the cannons and Gatling Guns Robert mentions.

North Albany County, WY, Homestead Years

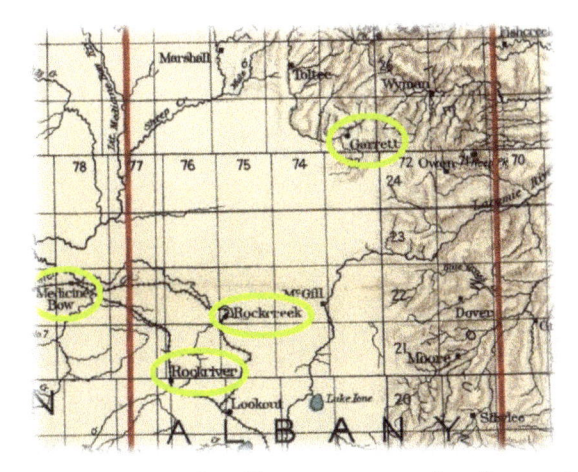

(1907 General Land Office Map, North Albany Co, WY around the time of the Slothower homesteading years. Garrett, Rock River, Rock Creek, Medicine Bow are shown)

Rock Creek, Wyoming
(From busy transportation hub to dust)

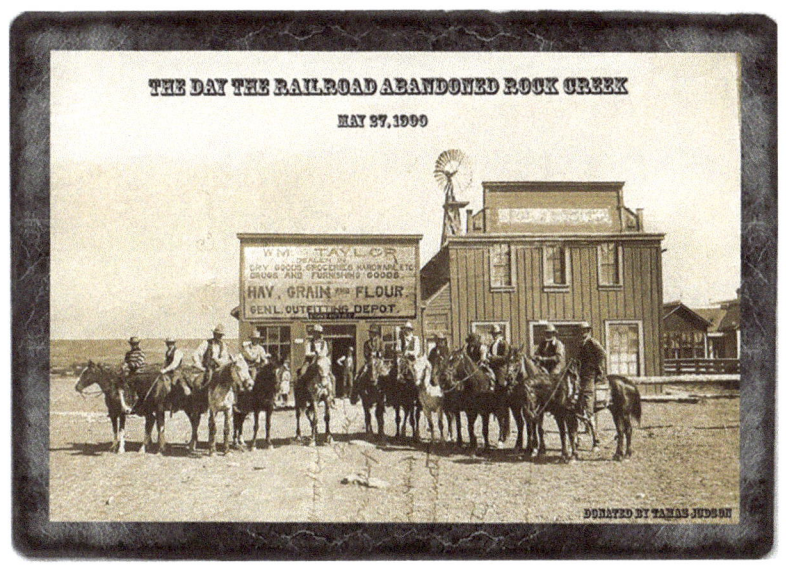

Rock Creek, WY, 1900, the day the railroad abandoned the town

(Black and white Rock Creek photos, courtesy of Dale Robbins of Marshall, Wyoming. Photographer unknown.)

William Taylor General Store and Warehouse above

Abandoned store and livery stable in Rock Creek, 1975 photo

William Taylor house in Rock Creek, 1897

(Color photos: Survey #: HABS WY-55, HABS WYO,1-ROCRI.V,1, Historic American Builds Survey, Library of Congress)

Robert and Elmer were first here in Rock Creek, Wyoming, in 1892. They were on their way to Aaron's homestead near Garrett. Robert mentions Rock Creek two or three times in his story. The colored pictures above were taken in 1975.

For anybody whose ancestors homesteaded in North Albany County, Rock Creek would have been a household name prior to 1905. I've learned that several of the Garrett area homesteaders worked in Rock Creek around the middle 1890s. Two of these would be T. S. Garrett and Carleton Skarratt. In many cases, this was during the time they were first developing their homesteads and building up their herds. Back then, the railroad went through Rock Creek, and the town was a major shipping hub for cattle. When the town was in its heyday in the mid-1880s and during cattle-shipping season, one hundred carloads of cattle would be shipped out every day. Then in 1900, the railroad abandoned the town moving farther southeast to Rock River, and the town started to die off after that.

Rock Creek was not only a transportation and shipping hub back in the day, but it had a "rough and tumble" side to it as well. It wasn't unusual for cowboys and freight drivers to frequent the local saloons to let off a little steam. Sometimes, the end result according to historical accounts is that someone got shot or got hung. Speaking of establishments, at its height, there were five saloons, a stockyard, a couple of hotels, two mercantiles, a school, but no churches.

Another important connection my great-grandfather had with Rock Creek was through a man by the name of Flake Hall. Robert talks about the Halls being good neighbors in the Garrett area and that Flake had been a personal friend of his, especially after his wife (Dollie) had died on the Wyoming homestead. Flake took over Robert's homestead on Cow Creek near Garrett right around 1910. This was when Robert left Wyoming for Southwest Washington State. The Halls also took over one of my great-grandfather's brands, the "76."

I believe it was sometime in the 1920s that Flake moved the main part of his cattle operation from Cow Creek to the abandoned town of Rock Creek. When I met the Garretts in July 2016, one of them told me that Flake had actually lived in the old abandoned town many years ago. The Halls still have descendants in the area. As a matter of fact, I met Flake's great-granddaughter, Maggie Peel, at the Rock River presentation in June of 2018. She also sent me a couple old photos of her great-grandparents. As a sidenote, I just happened to come across a real estate ad for the Hall Ranch in October of 2017. I hope the new owner appreciates the interesting history of this place.

I found an interesting article on the "Wyoming Tales and Trails" website about a discovery in Rock Creek that took place in 1909. This was back when my great-grandfather still lived in the area. A couple of men sent out to repair a collapsing wall in the cellar of an old store building inadvertently unearthed $4,177.50. The store had previously been operated by William Taylor. This was a lot of money back then! The discovery of the treasure, mostly in gold coin, has generated many theories as to the money's origin. Lots of rumors developed back in the day. Some said it may have come from a stage or train robbery, and the Wilcox train robbery was only a short distance away. Some even speculated that the money had been buried there by the notorious outlaw gang known as the Wild Bunch.

Photo of William Taylor (above) courtesy of Lillian Sako, Taylor's great-granddaughter

The money was found buried in a glass jar in the cellar floor. Shortly after the discovery, a dispute developed over entitlement, and the two men filed a lawsuit. Taylor claimed that he had buried the money in the 1890s when he was operating the store because the closest bank was some forty-seven miles away. The jury did not believe Taylor and the two men who had found the money felt victorious for a short while. However, this was not the end of it, and the case was brought before the Supreme Court where the case tried in the lower court was overturned, and Taylor received the booty.

In corresponding with one of Taylor's descendants, I learned that he had an interesting history besides the buried jar of money and the trials. Taylor served three years in the Wisconsin 1st Infantry during the Civil War. He carried a Henry rifle and was wounded during one of the battles. Taylor's first wife, Kate, died in Rock Creek leaving Taylor and two children behind. In addition to running a mercantile and a boarding house, Taylor mined bentonite near Rock Creek.

Based on some of my research and date of the colored photos, I got the impression that back in the 1970s, some of the old buildings of Rock Creek were still standing, and if you asked for permission, you could go in there and check out the old ghost town. However, things are not the same today as hardly a trace of the town remains, as shared with me by Dale Robbins of Marshall, Wyoming. When I visited North Albany County back in June of 2018, one of the locals told me that years ago, vandals burned down some of the remaining buildings. So little respect for history.

George Jordan, circa 1885 (source: American Heritage Center of Wyoming)

George Jordan's log cabin in North Albany County Wyoming. Above photograph likely taken in 1994 by John Ravage or Mark Harvey (source: Dale Robbins/Ranch History Project by Dicksie Knight May/American Heritage Center of Wyoming/ Ravage papers/Wyoming Black History Month). Below photograph courtesy of Amy Miller of Garrett, Wyoming, 2005)

My Great-grandfather Robert met George A. Jordan around 1900. Jordan was an African American homesteader from Kentucky and was born in 1866, one year after the Civil War ended. Robert didn't have an issue with Black folks and he and Jordan became friends. The two of them made several trips up into the mountains north of Garrett, Wyoming to get logs to build their cabins. On the last morning of their log gathering expedition, they woke up to a campsite covered with new snow. One of the cabins they built is pictured above and it is still standing today. The rest is described in the Wyoming chapter.

Great-grandfather Robert and the other area homesteaders (as I've been told) thought highly of Jordan. This was not always the case regarding the treatment of African Americans back in the very early 1900's. Jordan lived and worked at his homestead on Jordan Creek for fifty years before failing health forced his retirement. Jordan moved to Rock River, Wyoming in the 1940s and passed away in Laramie, Wyoming in 1949. Jordan never married and was one of the very few African American homesteaders in this part of Wyoming. George Jordan's story is also part of the John Ravage papers, which includes extensive research notes on black cowboys and black settlers of the United States.

(partially sourced from the American Heritage Center of Wyoming, February 22, 2017)

Country Wedding
Marriage of Mr. Slothower
and Miss Dollie Cameron

(Transcribed from February 5, 1902, the Laramie Republican)

Ceremony performed in the presence of a large number of guests who indulged in dance afterward and partook of a bountiful wedding supper. Handsome presents received by bride and groom.

Little Medicine, Wyoming, February 3 (special to the Republican) on Wednesday, the twenty-ninth of January, Mr. Robert J. Slothower of Garrett and Miss Dolly M. Cameron of Little Medicine were united in marriage in the home of the bride on Sheep Creek. Miss Maude Center acted as bridesmaid and Elmer G. Slothower as best man. Justice F. J. Banner performed the ceremony, which was witnessed by upward of sixty invited friends who attended from all directions.

The groom has been a resident of this county for the past eight years and is an upright and industrious young man. The bride has resided in the state but a short period, arriving from Colorado with her parents two years ago. She has qualities which, together with the groom's ability, will assure them success.

The wedding took place at 7:30 p.m., after which the musicians were requested to "tune up" and "do their best." The floor was at once crowded and continued so until daylight, with the exception of the interval for midnight supper. Mesdames Burnett, Marshall, Green, and Cameron, who were kept busy for two hours serving the sixty-five people with a bounteous feast, merited the praise they received from all for their efforts.

A few jigs and reels were performed by the boys, which gave the ladies a breathing spell, after which the dancing was resumed and was continued until daylight, when all partook of a lunch and hot coffee in preparation for a cold drive home.

The presents received were as follows:
Set dinner dishes—Little Medicine settlers.
Cookstove—Messrs. J. and G. Atkinson and Wm. Center.
Saddle horse—Ocie Center.
Clock—J. Newell Jr.
Silver butter knife—E. W. Green.
Pair bureau scarfs—Mr. and Mrs. Percy Newell.
Silk sofa cushion, biscuit pattern—Annie E. Cameron.

Silk sofa pillow, patch embroidered—Miss Maud Newell.
Bride's cake and stand—Mrs. Marshall.

Numerous other presents did not arrive in time for the wedding owing to the short notice.

The bride and groom were grateful and extended, thanks to all for assistance, as well as kind remembrance in the way of presents. The host and hostess, Mr. and Mrs. Cameron, should also be congratulated on their successful entertainment of so large a crowd.

Photo Section

Earliest known photograph of Robert J. Slothower taken in Denver, Colorado, age sixteen (Photo courtesy of Barbara Harman Higinbotham)

Robert J. Slothower, age mid- or late-twenties taken in Denver, Colorado, around 1898 (Photo courtesy of Lael Slothower Jenny)

Dollie Cameron Slothower
(Photo courtesy of Barbara Harman Higinbotham)
Robert's first wife died of acute appendicitis in 1909
on the homestead in Wyoming at age twenty-seven.

The above photo is of Dollie Cameron
(Robert Slothower's first wife) and Robert, sitting in
the rocking chair holding their new baby, Pearl.
Photo was taken on their homestead near
Garrett, Wyoming in 1904.

Robert, on right end, skinning a beef on his Cow Creek homestead with two other men from the Garrett, Wyoming community, circa 1906

Robert's cattle on winter feeding grounds, Cow Creek homestead, circa 1906

Bill Matheson, special friend of Robert's during the homestead years in Garrett, Wyoming. Photo courtesy of his granddaughter Carol Ackerman.

Robert Slothower's family in 1911
(Photo courtesy of Marie Nelson)
Starting over in Washington with new bride Leonia Martin.
In photo: Leonia, Robert, Pearl, Fred. Taken in Vancouver.

The Slothower triplets, born to Robert and Leonia: Walter, Eileen, and Charles. Birth date: August 10, 1912. (Above photos courtesy of Bea Settle)

Robert and Leonia's triplets are twenty-two years old in this photo. (Left to right) Charles, Eileen, and Walter. Photo accompanied an article that celebrated their uniqueness as being among the very few triplets to be born in the greater Vancouver area to date. Source, Vancouver, WA newspaper, 1934.

*Robert J. Slothower family portrait taken around 1929–30
Front row: Fred, Leonia, Robert (Sr.), Pearl (holding
daughter, Barbara Harman), Robert Slothower (Gray).
Back row: Charles, Eileen, and Walter (The triplets).
(Photo courtesy of Barbara Harman Higinbotham)*

This photograph would have been especially dear to the family as Eileen died at twenty-three and left a husband and two daughters behind and Robert Jr. was raised by his Aunt May in Colorado away from the rest of the family. Robert Jr. also died young; he passed away at age thirty-five.

Lewis B. Slothower (Robert's father). Probably taken in Denver, Colorado, around 1895 (Photo courtesy of Maxine Slothower Sullivan)

Robert's parents, Lewis and Eliza Slothower. This picture was taken in Denver, Colorado, around 1905. (Photo courtesy of Lael Jenny and Dennis Slothower)

Old Slothower family Bible given to me (Jay Harman) by Barbara Harman Higinbotham. It had belonged to Robert, and he had written his siblings' names and birthdays inside the front cover. (Jay Harman photo)

Aaron Slothower (Robert's older brother), age about twenty. Photo probably taken in Denver, circa 1888. (Photo courtesy of Donna Slothower Hornsby)

Edith Slothower at about age twenty, circa 1889. (Photo courtesy of Bea Slothower Settle)

Elmer Slothower (Robert's younger brother) about age twenty-two. Circa 1895 in Cheyenne, Wyoming. (Photo courtesy of Barbara Higinbotham)

Photo of Robert's youngest sibling Cora, at about age twenty. Photo taken in Denver, CO around 1895.

Edith Slothower's baby girl (Paulina Marsh) born in 1891 in Pueblo, CO. Edith's husband died in 1894 at age twenty-five and little Paulina died the following year at age four. In 1910 Edith married Charles Hone. Photo courtesy of Bea Settle

Robert, Jr. age four, at the A. Gray homestead, CO, 1913

Aaron Slothower, Robert's older brother, age thirty-six, (Grand Encampment Herald photo, 1903, Encampment, Wyoming)

Aaron, Edith, Robert, Elmer, and Cora, taken in 1944 in Felida at Slothower Family Reunion (Photo courtesy of Maxine Sullivan)

Cora Slothower's family. Top row, Bob Fortune, Cora Slothower Johnson, Hazel Fortune. Bottom row, Arthur Fortune, and Mary Fortune Grant. Photo taken in Denver, CO in about 1912.

Cora was Robert's youngest sibling and her family is shown above. In the Denver chapter Robert mentions that his younger sister Cora, had a good life as a child, but that all changed when she married a "whiskey bum" at age sixteen. Things got so bad with her alcoholic husband that around 1900 three of her children were placed in an orphanage in Denver. Things must have improved later because she got them back. In recent years there has been some speculation in the extended family that there may be some Native American ancestry in this branch of the family tree. However, nothing concrete has surfaced to back this up. Just one more family mystery.

Cora's oldest child, Bob, was good with horses, having worked on ranches in Wyoming before serving in an army veterinary hospital in France during the last year of WWI. Once back in the states, Bob returned to work on ranches north of Rock River, Wyoming and this was his occupation for about the next twenty years. Several years later when he was in his fifties, he married a woman from Texas, and then two years after that he committed suicide. There were more hard times to come for this part of the family when Cora's youngest child, Arthur, was convicted of first degree robbery in California in 1935. Arthur served time in San Quentin Prison, was paroled in 1938, and committed suicide a year later. Both of Cora's daughters entered their first marriage at around age sixteen, same as their mother.

Martha and William Cameron standing in front of their farmhouse in Brush Prairie, Washington, about 1910. (Photo courtesy of Bea Settle)

The Camerons (Dollie Slothower's parents) had left Wyoming sometime in 1908, prior to Dollie's death. They had moved to Brush Prairie, a farming community north of Vancouver, Washington. This had a role in Robert's decision to take a look at the farming area west of Vancouver, Washington, after Dollie's death. Dollie, as readers probably recall, was Robert's first wife, and she died of acute appendicitis on the homestead in Wyoming.

Dollie Slothower's parents, Martha and William Cameron. William was a Union Army Civil War veteran (Photo courtesy of Bea Settle)

*Harvey Cameron, Dollie Cameron's youngest brother.
(Courtesy of Marie Nelson)*

Harvey was involved in his family's ranching business and was part of the Marshall, Wyoming community from about 1900 to 1910. Then he left for Brush Prairie, Washington, to join his parents. Photo taken in about 1925 in Vancouver, Washington.

Left to right, Lillis Bishop Cameron, then two of Dollie's brothers, James Cameron, Harvey Cameron, Albert Gray, May Cameron Gray (who raised Robert Jr.) Photo probably taken in Northern Colorado on the Gray homestead circa 1910.

*Martha Cameron (Dollie's mother)
Photo probably taken in Colorado in about 1898
(Photo courtesy of Barbara Higinbotham)*

Robert Slothower and daughter Eileen on hike up Beacon Rock on Columbia River, circa 1924. (Photo courtesy of Marie Nelson)

Pearl Slothower, mid-1930s at Lake Pleasant, Washington. (Above and below photo courtesy of Carol Harman)

James R. Harman, my (Jay Harman's) father, and Pearl Slothower Harman. Photos taken in about 1950 in Port Angles, Washington.

Robert's oldest son, Fred Slothower, senior picture, 1924, Vancouver, WA

Fred Slothower, Robert's oldest son, with his dog Queenie, taken in mid-1930s at Lake Pleasant, Washington. (Photo courtesy of Carol Harman)

The above images represent a trip Robert and Leonia took Robert Jr. on in early September of 1929. They went up on the Olympic Peninsula in Washington State to visit Robert's oldest daughter, Pearl Slothower Harman (my grandmother). Pearl was raising a two-year-old daughter and teaching school in a one-room schoolhouse outside of Port Angeles. A recently discovered entry in a ninety-year-old guest book found in the family's Lake Crescent cabin sheds light on the visit. After reading Robert Jr.'s entry, it was easy to see that he was taken with the natural beauty of the place and the Harman hospitality. Readers may recall that Robert Sr. hadn't seen his second oldest son for nineteen years, so no doubt this was a very special trip.

Canol Pipeline - ALCAN Highway
Oil for Victory - WWII

Robert Slothower Jr. began working on the Canol Project in the Yukon Territory, Canada in April of 1943. He died a year later in Lethbridge, Alberta. Black and white photo shows Canol pipeline welding crew in action. The welding machines were housed in improvised tents on sleds towed by tractors. January 15, 1944. YUKON ARCHIVES. FINNIE FAMILY FONDS, 81/21 #465, PHO 141.

Robert Jr. was on the track-and-field team while attending Ft. Collins High School in Colorado. They were state champions in 1925 and 1926. I believe he did either the shot put or the discus. As the story goes, Robert was offered a college scholarship, but turned them down. Robert Jr. died after surgery on his appendix in April of 1944, at the age of thirty-five. His mother (Dollie Cameron Slothower) died from appendicitis on the remote homestead in Wyoming when Robert, Jr. was just one year old.

Above photo shows Robert Jr. in track uniform.
Photo taken in Colorado in about 1926.
(Photo courtesy of Bea Settle)

Robert and Leonia's triplets

*Walter Slothower, probably his senior photo from high school.
Photo probably taken around 1929 or 1930.
(Photo courtesy of Bea Settle)*

*Eileen, one of the triplets. Photo taken in Vancouver, Washington.
Eileen died young, as had Robert Jr., at age twenty-three
(Photo courtesy of Bea Settle)*

*Charles, one of the triplets. Photo taken in Vancouver
Charles was an artist and a painter.
(Photo courtesy of Bea Settle)*

*Robert's prune dryer and children (on left)
in Felida, Washington, 1916
(Photo courtesy of Bea Settle)*

*Robert's children in his Felida farm prune orchard, circa 1918
(Photo courtesy of Bea Settle)*

*Robert with granddaughter Bea Slothower
on the Felida farm, circa 1943
(Photo courtesy of Bea Settle)*

Felida farmhouse in 1952
(Above and below photos, courtesy of Bea Settle)

Old Felida School northwest of Vancouver, Washinton. Built in 1896. This is where all of Robert's children (except for Robert Jr.) attended grade school beginning the fall of 1910. Source: Felida Elementary website, 2018.

Leonia with granddaughters (Eileen's daughters), date unknown.

Pearl, Robert's oldest, picking berries near the Felida farm in about 1920. Age around sixteen (Photo courtesy of Barbara Higinbotham)

Robert, Leonia, and oldest son Fred in Kennewick, Washington, at their son Fred's fuel business in 1952. This is the last known photo of Robert Slothower. He died later that same year. (Photo courtesy of Marie Nelson)

Robert's Brothers

From Wyoming to Washington

ROBERT

AARON

ELMER

SLOTHOWER BROTHERS
GARRETT, WY 1892

Aaron Slothower

Aaron was Robert's older brother, and he was exceptional in his own right. Aaron was born on October 12, 1867 in Harrisburg, Pennsylvania. This was two years after the Civil War ended and shortly before the family started to migrate west. In Robert's story, it's easy to tell that Aaron, even as a young man, had a knack for inventing things, was a hard worker, and became independent and a bit of an "adventure seeker." He is also the perfect example of someone who participated in the "Great Westward Migration" starting in Pennsylvania and winding up in Vancouver, Washington, and living in a total of eight states as he worked his way west.

I was surprised to come across a record that said Arron had married a woman in Denver in June of 1891 by the name of Maud Metcalf. A cousin of mine told me that Aaron's first wife was a French "Saloon Girl," so this must have been her. He must have married her shortly before he headed to Wyoming, but the marriage didn't last. I found an old Wyoming newspaper clipping that gave the most recent court cases (of that time), and it gave Aaron and Maud's name in the divorce cases bracket. It also stated that the grounds for divorce was desertion, so it gives the impression that Aaron's first wife couldn't handle the rough, isolated homestead life in the remote hills of Wyoming.

I don't have a lot of information on Aaron, but I can tell you that he was the first brother to come out to Wyoming to homestead near Garrett, and this was in about 1891. In Robert's story, he tells of coming out to join his two brothers, Aaron and Elmer, at Arron's ranch in April of 1892. Robert also states that Aaron's place is about one mile south of his place on Cow Creek. The first couple years Aaron was on Cow Creek, he grew hay and potatoes, but wasn't interested in raising cattle. Aaron never received his homestead patent on his place but turned his squatter's rights over to Robert in about 1896.

After leaving Cow Creek, Aaron headed for the Encampment area where there was a lot of mining activity; this was in 1896–97. Aaron was the first resident of the little mining town of Rambler which was close to Battle Lake and way up high near the Continental Divide. In December 1902, Aaron married Ruth Martin from Colorado. This is the same year Robert got married farther north in Albany County, Wyoming. Aaron's marriage to Ruth was also significant because some years later after losing his first wife, Robert married Ruth's sister, Leonia. In other words, two brothers married two sisters. The Martins (Ruth and Leonia's family) had done well in the silver mining business in Colorado before coming to Carbon County, Wyoming. When I visited Park Hill Cemetery in Vancouver, Washington in July of 2019, I saw that brothers Aaron and Robert were buried right next to one another along with their Martin wives, so in an earthly and spiritual sense, they will be close to one another through eternity.

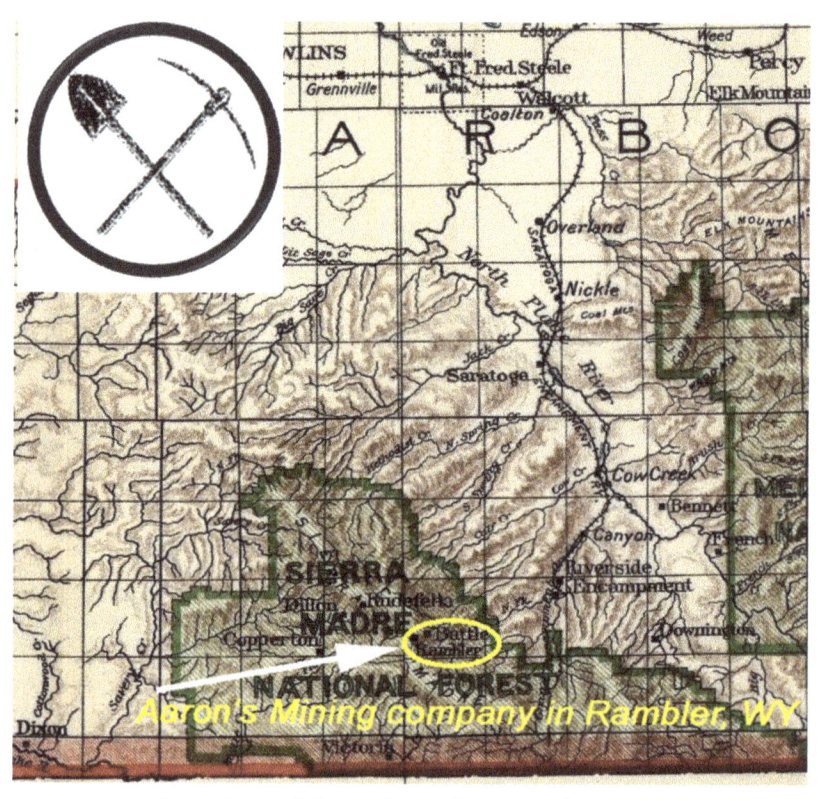

Location of Aaron's residence and mining company in Rambler, Wyoming, beginning in 1897 (General Land Office Map of 1907)

Aaron Slothower and Ruth Martin 1902 marriage certificate. It was a double wedding. The other couple was Leslie Niece and Ellen Martin (Ruth's sister). Courtesy Donna S. Hornsby

Ruth Martin Slothower (Aaron's wife) holding baby Louis. Probably taken in Encampment, Wyoming. Photo taken circa 1904. Courtesy of Donna Slothower Hornsby.

I came across a newspaper article that said Aaron and Ruth lost their first child in May 1906. This was while they were still living in Rambler. It was a little boy (Louis) only two and a half years old when he died, and he had been sickly since birth. He's buried in the cemetery in Encampment.

Historic newspaper articles and mining records indicate that mining became Aaron's primary interest from about 1897 to 1910. However, the *Daily Boomerang* (no. 236 December 19, 1894, page 3) states that Aaron partnered with T. S. Garrett to create the North Laramie Mines in Northern Albany County near Laramie Peak and that the prospects for the mine looked very good at the time. This was not very far from the where the three Slothower brothers had their homesteads near Garrett. I couldn't find anything that stated if this venture was successful, but I have a hunch that it didn't pan out because two years after this, Aaron moved to Rambler and T. S. Garrett stayed in the cattle business.

I also discovered that Aaron dabbled in politics when he was elected to be Rambler's delegate to some big miners' meeting in Encampment, and he also ran for justice of the peace for North Laramie County (around Garrett) before that.

Even though he had his own mines, he and his partner in Rambler did contract work for other people who owned mines. In addition, Aaron partnered with a man named Porter, and they had a store and the mail and stage stop in Rambler.

Stagecoach at Encampment, Wyoming.
(Photo by Rock Mountain Studio in Encampment)
(Also Thorpe Collection, P69-25/590B, WY State Archives)

Aaron became an important figure in the mining business around 1903. By this time, Rambler had about 175 residents, two hotels, one general store, a post office, and one saloon with a gaming fraternity (gambling club). Aaron promoted mining in the area around Rambler (including his own mining operation), and he promoted the town itself and the prospects for the biggest mining operation in the immediate area which was the Doan Rambler Mine.

The other thing that I began to realize after conducting more research was that this part of Wyoming from about 1898 to 1908 was in the midst of the big "Copper Boom." As a result, there was a lot of investment in the area and a lot of mining-related construction going on. Some of these projects were major engineering feats. The big smelter in Encampment, the four foot in diameter pipeline that delivered water from miles away to power the project, and the sixteen-mile-long tramway were impressive. The tramway went over the Continental Divide at an elevation of 10,700 feet and was the longest in the world at the time!

(Source for above: Wyoming State Historic Preservation Office)

Tramway going from mining area to Encampment Smelter. Buckets suspended from heavy-duty cables could each hold up to seven hundred pounds of copper ore. Smelter visible in background.
Stimson Collection, STIM/762, WY State Archives, 1903 photo

Pipeline crossing river to Encampment Smelter, circa 1903 (Source for above: Wyoming Tales and Trails, Geoffrey Dobson)

The pipeline, made of wood and metal hoops, took water from the south fork of the Grand Encampment River four miles away to the copper smelter at Encampment. There, the water drove five turbine wheels, two of which were connected to the shafting and drive for the heavy machinery; the other three provided electric power. I'm sure my great-uncle Aaron loved all these engineering marvels, considering he was a builder and a bit of an inventor himself.

1903 photo of smelter in Encampment. Large smelter was used to process copper ore that came from area mines, including Rambler (Stimson Collection, STIM/765, Wyoming State Archives)

*Rambler, Wyoming, circa 1900
(Courtesy of James Perue, Wyoming. Early
History of the Cowboy State)*

Battle Pass USFS sign. Source: passbagger. org, Randy Bishop, 2011

Rambler Wyoming, winter 1904 (Wyoming Tales and Trails)

Most people have no idea how cold and how deep the snow gets in winter in this part of the country. The elevation at the Rambler site is 9,200 feet. Rambler is about fifteen miles southwest of Encampment in the Sierra Madre Range and not far from the Continental Divide.

Rambler, Wyoming, 1907
(Wyoming Tales and Trails)

The old townsite of Rambler sits just north of historic and pristine Battle Lake and is close to the Sierra Madre National Forest, but is actually on private land. It's impressive to think that Aaron started a town from scratch, even though the town didn't last. There is virtually no sign of the town today, except for possibly the old artesian well that once served the original town. However, I did learn from a fellow member on one of the Wyoming history sites, that (a few years ago) the remains of some of the old miners' cabins were still standing. It is still a beautiful mountainous area with good hiking and fishing.

Nellie Martin Dettinger (Aaron and Robert's sister-in-law) on horse with baby, circa 1913. Probably taken on Dettinger homestead north of Encampment, WY. Photo courtesy of Marie Nelson

The Copper Handbook

A MANUAL OF THE COPPER INDUSTRY OF THE WORLD

VOL. VII

COMPILED AND PUBLISHED BY
HORACE J. STEVENS
HOUGHTON, MICH., U. S. A.
1907

RAMBLER MINING CO.   **WYOMING.**

Office and mine: Rambler, Carbon Co., Wyo. Idle. S. H. Potter, president; Aaron Slothower, treasurer and general manager; L. S. Niece, secretary. Organized under laws of Wyoming, with capitalization $2,000,000, shares $1 par. Lands, 9 claims, area 160 acres, in the Battle Lake district, showing veins occurring as fissures in diabase schists and as contacts between diabase and quartzite, veins ranging 1' to 6' in width, and giving assays up to 25% copper and $1 to $10 gold per ton, from oxide, carbonate and sulphide ores. Development is by a 100' main shaft and a 550' crosscut tunnel. Idle for several years.

Will Martin (Aaron's brother-in-law) winning Rock Drilling Contest, Encampment, 1904.

Battle Lake, Wyoming, 2017
(Courtesy of Western United Realty in Laramie, Wyoming)

Before the tramway was completed, the mines in the area had to transport their ore sixteen miles by mule team to Encampment where they had built a large smelter. The mines did well for about ten years, then there was a second big fire at the smelter in Encampment, then problems with financiers, then the bottom fell out of the copper market. As a result, the mining companies and towns fell on hard times. By 1910, most of the people had left. As of 1941, most of Rambler had fallen down, and it had become a ghost town. Aaron moved there in 1897, and he stayed there until about 1906 or 1907. Then Aaron moved to Stanley, Idaho, to pursue new mining opportunities in the beautiful Sawtooth Mountains. However, the 1910 federal census lists his occupation as carpenter, not miner. Based on my research, he did both.

Mule teams hauling copper from Encampment smelter, 1903 photo. (Frank Meyers Collection, American Heritage Center, University of Wyoming)

The following photo shows one of the tunnels in the Ferris-Haggarty Mine. This was the largest and most productive mine in the Encampment District and not far from Rambler where Aaron lived and had his base of operations.

Mine supervisors assessing heavy timbers inside the Osceola tunnel of the Ferris-Haggarty Mine in the Grand Encampment Mining District of Southern Wyoming. (By J. E. Stimson, STIM/752, Wyoming Division of State Parks and Cultural Res)

Battle, Wyoming, 1904
(Cities & Towns—Battle WY #1, 7103, Wyoming State Archives)

    Battle was another little mining town just a short distance from Rambler but a little higher up and as about as close to the Continental Divide as you can get. Aaron had a patent for his own mine in the Battle Lake District, and it was called the Big Divide Lode. There were over a hundred mines in the area at the time. The mines in the Battle Lake Mining District for the most part were named for the creeks and gulches in the area: Doane Creek, Haggerty Creek, and so on.

    Both Battle and Rambler were exceptionally high in elevation, so to say they were a bit frosty in the wintertime would be an understatement. It was not at all unusual for these little mining towns to receive four to six feet of snow during the winter. In some of the pictures of the miners' living quarters, it looked like they were digging out of snow caves.

Miners' children southwest of Encampment. The little girl sitting in the box is Leonia Martin. She would become Robert Slothowers second wife in 1911. Photo circa 1899, courtesy of Marie Nelson.

The Office Saloon in Battle, Wyoming in winter of 1902 (Ledbetter Collection—Album Vol. 1, H66- 78/31, WY State Archives)

In his "life story," Robert said that Aaron wasn't much of a drinker, but I'm guessing that some of the other miners didn't mind having a "watering hole" to frequent, especially during the snowy winter months. Note that the man (second in from the left) is holding his dog up for the photo.

Stanley, Idaho. William Solue photograph taken in about 1924.

Maxine Sullivan, one of Aaron's granddaughters, told me that Aaron took his sons back to Stanley, Idaho, when they were in their teen years. Aaron was there from about 1907 to about 1910.

Ruth, Aaron's wife, gave birth to their third son while they were living in Stanley. Aaron was an adventurous man and seemed to be attracted to rugged, mountainous, remote, and beautiful places.

Elmer Slothower

Elmer was Robert's younger brother, and he was born in 1873 in Phillips County, Kansas, near the frontier town of Marvin (now Glade). He was the fourth child born to Lewis and Eliza Slothower. He spent the first few years of his life growing up in Kansas on the prairie homestead living initially in the sod house, then briefly in the stone house his father had built. When times got tough and his father could no longer make a living off the land, his parents left for Colorado, and he was given up to be raised by a neighboring farm family. He stayed with them for about seven years.

Some childhood stories (both informational and entertaining) can be found in Robert's life story, so I won't recap those in this summary. In about 1888, he boarded a train with his brother Robert and headed west for Colorado to join the rest of the family and for about the next four years he lived in Denver. He left Denver for Wyoming around 1891 or 1892. The 1900 census record shows that Elmer, at age twenty-seven, was in North Laramie. Elmer was tall (at least 6' 3" and at least 220 pounds), sturdily built, and he knew how to work. His Garrett homestead document shows that he received his patent in 1903, but he actually started building his ranch about four years before that. Elmer was the first of the brothers to receive a patent for his homestead.

Elmer married Elvira Nelson from Rock River in December 1905. Elvira was the daughter of Fremont Nelson, a prominent rancher from Rock River. His first three children (Elmer Jr., Edith, and Ruth) were born either in Rock River or on the homestead in Garrett, but they were living on the Garrett homestead at the time. These children were born in 1907, 1909, and 1910.

Elmer's 1903 Homestead Document

In 1911 Elmer sold his homestead to Walter Roe and may have left Wyoming with his family at that time. He was in Felida, Washington, in 1916, as his daughter, Mary, was born there that year. This may have been at his brother Robert's place since Robert lived in Felida at the time. Then they moved to West Dalles, Oregon. The 1920 census indicates that he lived on a farm and listed his occupation as rural mail carrier. However, he returned to the Nelson ranch in Rock River, Wyoming (his mother-in-law's place) around 1922 and stayed there for about the next seventeen years.

The 1930 census indicates that he lived in the small town of Rock River and gives his occupation as carpenter. However, he may have split his time between working on the Nelson ranch which was just one mile east of Rock River and doing carpentry work in town. He left Wyoming for good around 1938 or 1939 and went to Clark County Washington to join other family members, including his brothers Aaron and Robert. He and Elvira settled in a rural farming community called Orchards located north of Vancouver, Washington, and they spent the rest of their years there. Elmer died in 1964 and is buried in Vancouver, Washington. Elmer and Elvira had nine children who survived to adulthood.

While homesteading in Wyoming, he raised cattle and hay. His special talents were playing the fiddle, composing music, building his own instruments, and gardening. He also engineered an amazing irrigation system while homesteading on the North Laramie River near Garrett, Wyoming.

Elmer and Robert were close as brothers, and each had a homestead near Garrett in the very early 1900s. Once you've read the "Wyoming" section of Robert's life story, it becomes very apparent that the two brothers had a great relationship through good times and bad. During the homestead years, there were times when they worked together on construction and ranch projects, helped one another out in time of need, provided entertainment at the "old time" country dances with their fiddle and guitar. And in time of crisis, such as when Dollie came down with appendicitis, it was Elmer who went out into a winter blizzard with just a horse and a buckboard to fetch the doctor many miles away. Elmer was the best man at Robert and Dollie's wedding in Wyoming in January 1902.

Elmer Slothower family and Fremont Nelson family portrait. Elmer, second in from right middle row; Elvira (Elmer's wife) in back row, center, holding baby. Mary Nelson, bottom left-hand corner; Fremont Nelson, bottom row, right end, holding little girl.

Photo taken in 1911 in Wyoming, courtesy of Janice Dugan

Below photo, Elmer's favorite violin
(Photo courtesy of Janice Dugan)

Elmer was a talented musician and, like his brother Robert, was self-taught and built his own instruments. I was told that Elmer may have built as many as twenty-five violins from scratch and that he still played even into his senior years. Elmer even composed some of his own songs and sold them to a music company in Denver. Elmer played the fiddle, and Robert played the guitar. Elmer and Robert became very popular around Garrett, and they played at many of the "old time" country dances. They even played at a surprise party in March of 1902 for local "pioneer legend" Frank Prager. Prager was one of the first pioneers to settle in this part of Wyoming. His ranch was on the southeast side of Laramie Peak, not far from Elmer's homestead. Prager was not only well-known and respected as one of the earliest ranchers, but was also a renowned Indian fighter in earlier years.

Frank and Rosa Prager; photo taken in 1882. Wyoming State Archives.

I came across a January 1907 newspaper article from the *Laramie Republican* that was too entertaining to not include. Elmer and his wife (Elvira) attended this dance, and Elmer probably played his fiddle there as well. Evidently, there was an incident involving some sheepherders crashing the gathering on the William Atkinson Ranch near what used to be McGill north of Rock River. The Atkinsons were celebrating the completion of a new bunkhouse. There's a very good chance that Robert helped to build the bunkhouse as he had built a number of other structures for the Atkinsons. I shared this little story back in June when I gave my presentation in Rock River.

The social gathering (of primarily cattle ranchers) was going very well from the previous evening almost until the next morning. Back in the day, these country dances lasted way into the night, and it wasn't unusual for guests to depart the following morning. Shortly before daybreak, the harmonious festivities were interrupted when three crazy sheepherders crashed the party and threatened to break up the dance. However, some of the cowboys came up with a solution and told the sheepherders that if they settled down, they could sit in the corner and look on.

When the ranch's foreman came in and assessed the situation, he decided that it would be a good idea to put up a temporary fence to keep the two groups from mixing. Then one of the cowboys accidentally ran into the fence and peeled off a few inches of hide from his face. Of course, this triggered a serious confrontation between the cowboy and the foreman even though they were both nonsheepmen. The foreman, hoping to avoid a fight, used his negotiating skills to calm the angry, revenge-seeking cowboy. Then the sheepherders left, and the cowboys removed the fence, and the dancing continued until morning. I guess you could say that "All's well that ends well in the early days of North Albany County."

In visiting with one of Elmer's granddaughters (Janice Dugan) in 2017, I learned some additional interesting things about Elmer. She reflected on a conversation from many years ago when she was talking to him about faith and God. From this conversation, Janice got the impression that her grandfather may have not been a man of faith because he said that he didn't know about heaven, but that he did know about hell because he had been there. Thinking about the years of separation from his family during his childhood years in Kansas and the harsh winters he experienced in Wyoming during the homestead years, this made perfect sense to me.

I was also told that there was a tragic event during his Rock River years when a little girl got lost in a snowstorm on her way home from school. Elmer was a member of the search party. Unfortunately, this had a very sad ending due to the extreme weather conditions, and the little girl froze to death.

Moving on to more recent times, I had a very surprising encounter at the Rock River presentation in June 2018. I met a ninety-five-year old lady who had attended the Rock River School with some of Elmer's children back around the mid-1930s. She remembered a Halloween prank that one of Elmer's sons and some other boys were involved with. Evidentially, they found a goat somewhere and somehow were able to put it up on the roof at the school. She went on to say that it was the "talk of the town" for a while.

Rock River High School, 1938
(Courtesy of Janice Dugan)

Several of Elmer's kids went to high school in Rock River while they lived in Wyoming from about 1922 to about 1938. After their time in Rock River, the family picked up and moved to a small community called Orchards, a short distance northeast of Vancouver, Washington. It was only a few years after Elmer's family moved to Orchards that the United States entered World War II. Two of Elmer and Elvira's children, Robert and Barney, served in the military during this time. Barney received a Purple Heart for getting wounded in Okinawa. This happened when Barney's unit was advancing on an enemy position. Barney took two rounds from a Japanese machine gun.

In 2016, one of my aunts who knew Robert many years ago told me that in the late 1930s and 1940s, Robert would occasionally talk Leonia (Robert's second wife) into going over to Elmer's for a visit. Leonia, being rather religious and straitlaced would hesitate a bit and then agree to go. I guess it wasn't unusual for there to be a fair amount of commotion going on over at Elmer's; after all, he and Elvira had nine kids.

(In the above photo are three of Elmer Slothower's children in front of the La Bonte Canyon homestead log cabin. From left to right is Edith, Ruth and Johnnie Slothower. Photo was taken in about 1933.)

It's important to note that it wasn't just the men who made wonderful contributions during the homestead days. Elmer's oldest daughter, Edith, was a tough homesteading individual same as some of the others. She married Roy B. Patrick in about 1926. Roy (a World Word I veteran) had been homesteading as early as 1917 in LaBonte Canyon. Roy built a log cabin, raised horses, and cultivated some of the land down in the bottom of the canyon along the creek.

Roy and Edith raised five children together. Talk about a rugged and remote place to raise five kids! Their homestead totaled just over 1,300 acres. The old Patrick homestead is now part of the Medicine Bow National Forest. Robert (in the Wyoming chapter) talks about trying to cross LaBonte Canyon in the dark to find his brother Elmer.

Roy B. Patrick with his children (Elmer Slothower's grandchildren) on LaBonte Canyon, Wyoming homestead. Photo taken circa 1936. Courtesy of Glenda Cates.

The above photo was taken on the LaBonte homestead in about 1933. Elemer Slothower on horse with son-in-law Roy Patrick, holding the reins.

Elemer Slothower at his home in Orchards, WA, 1940's

Pictured in the above photo are (sitting, left to right) family friend Tex, then Slothower family members Elmer and June; (standing, left to right) Irene, Elvira, Mary, and Barney. Photo circa 1939 in Orchards, WA.

Elmer left a living legacy with his handmade fiddles that have been passed down through the generations. One descendant, Glenda Cates, has been looking for the "Rough Riders" song, written by Elmer and published by the Tolbert Ingram Music Company in 1905. She hopes to have her grandson play it on one of Elmer's fiddles.

Elmer and Elvira were "salt of the earth" people and didn't have a lot in the way of financial resources, but they had a lot of love for their family, a wonderful garden during the summer, and some of the best "well water" in the Orchards community.

Elvira Nelson Slothower (Elmer's wife on left end) Elmer Slothower (holding baby) and Robert Slothower on far right end. Rock River, WY, circa 1928. Photo courtesy of Marie Nelson

Trips to the Wyoming Homesteads

First Trip to the Wyoming Homesteads
July 2016

[Source: Wyoming BLM map]

It was great to have the opportunity to go to great-grandfather Robert's homestead in the summer of 2016. I was fortunate that my brother, John, was able to go with me, especially considering that the round-trip was about 2,350 miles!

We also got lucky and just happened to catch the rancher who now owns Great-uncle Elmer's old homestead ranch. Both homesteads are near a little spot in the road called Garrett. Trust me, this place is very remote; some Wyoming maps don't even show it. However, it is beautiful and probably doesn't look a whole lot different from how it looked back in 1910, the year my great-grandfather left Wyoming.

Another very interesting thing about the ranchers around Garrett is that descendants of many of the "old time" ranching families are still there! Many of these families were mentioned in Robert's life story. It was kind of like stepping back in time. I should also mention that they were very welcoming, and John and I appreciated that.

Origins of the Journey

As you no doubt realize by now, the motivation for this long trek all started with Robert's story and further discovery of my Slothower ancestors. My anticipation grew even greater because I'd never been to this part of Wyoming before. In addition, this would be my first opportunity to meet some of the descendants of homesteaders mentioned in Robert's story. The heart of this amazing trip was about making these connections. As mentioned earlier, Robert and Elmer were two brothers who came out from Denver, Colorado, in about 1892 to join their oldest brother Aaron, who had a homestead and built a cabin up along Cow Creek in the hills just northwest of Garrett.

(Laramie Peak Photo by Karina Lewis 2015)

Elmer Slothower and Elvira Nelson (pictured below) were married in December 1905. Elvira was Fremont Nelson's daughter. Fremont was an early homesteader and prominent rancher from Rock River.

Portrait photos of Elmer and Elvira taken in Wyoming in 1911
(Photo courtesy of Janice Dugan)

Robert and Dollie Slothower
(Photo on right courtesy of Barbara Harman Higinbotham)

The above picture of Robert is from about 1896. The one of Dollie had to be prior to December 1909 because that is when she died on the homestead on Cow Creek in Wyoming.

Robert started working on his homestead on Cow Creek in about 1901. He and Dollie Cameron were married at the Cameron homestead near Marshall in January 1902.

Accession	Names	Date	Doc #	State	Meridian	Twp - Rng	Aliquots	Sec. #	County
22518	SLOTHOWER, DOLLY M 80 Acres Desert Land Act GARRETT Wife of Robert J.	10/15/1908	1700	WY	6th PM	025N - 074W	SE¼NE¼	13	Albany
						025N - 074W	NE¼SE¼	13	Albany
WYWYAA 009311	SLOTHOWER, ELMER 160 Acres Homestead Entry Original GARRETT	5/19/1903	1619	WY	6th PM	025N - 073W	E½SE¼	21	Albany
						025N - 073W	NW¼SW¼	22	Albany
						025N - 073W	NE¼NE¼	28	Albany
MV-0697-290	SLOTHOWER, ELMER G 120 Acres Desert Land Act GARRETT Brother to Robert J.	12/9/1907	1570	WY	6th PM	025N - 073W	S½NE¼	22	Albany
						025N - 073W	SE¼NW¼	22	Albany
WYWYAA 009322	SLOTHOWER, ELMER G SAME AS ABOVE	12/9/1907	1570	WY	6th PM	025N - 073W	S½NE¼	22	Albany
						025N - 073W	SE¼NW¼	22	Albany
47901	SLOTHOWER, ROBERT J 80 Acres Sale-Cash Entry GARRETT	2/23/1909	0814	WY	6th PM	025N - 074W	NW¼SE¼	13	Albany
						025N - 074W	SW¼SE¼	13	Albany
WYWYAA 009316	SLOTHOWER, ROBERT J 167.37 Acres Homestead Entry Original GARRETT	4/14/1906	1979	WY	6th PM	025N - 074W	NE¼NE¼	13	Albany
						025N - 073W	Lot/Trct 1	18	Albany
						025N - 073W	Lot/Trct 2	18	Albany

(Courtesy of Dicksie Knight May, Albany County Historical Society and the Bureau of Land Management, GLO Records)

I received the previous document from the Albany County Historical Society. It shows the Slothower homesteads. Unfortunately, I haven't been able to locate any records for Aaron's homestead and now realize that's because he never received his patent. However, after reviewing the Wyoming section of Robert's life story, I did figure out the location of it. Aaron's homestead was about a mile down Cow Creek (south) from where Robert's was. Regardless of the patent issue, Aaron still worked his homestead for at least four years, and I was curious about the cabin he had built there.

Back to the trip.

*Wind machines on the way to Medicine Bow
(Jay Harman photo, July 2016)*

It took us two days to get to Medicine Bow from Western Oregon; this was the closest town to Garrett with a decent motel. We had been told that there were good motels in Wheatland, but we never made it that far east. Robert mentions Medicine Bow in his life story. *Bow*, as the locals call it, was quite a town back in the day. Back in the late 1800s and early 1900s, it was a transportation hub with the railroad, a destination for ranchers who had cattle to sell. Now there isn't much to "Bow," just a remnant of what it once was due to a new highway route being constructed farther south several years ago.

The famous book entitled The Virginian *has its roots in Medicine Bow. This is displayed in the bar that is on the lower level of the old Virginian Hotel. (Jay Harman photo July 2016)*

Virginian Hotel in Medicine Bow, Wyoming, 2016 photo (Jay Harman photo, July 2016)

The Virginian Hotel in Medicine Bow, 1911
(Wyoming Tales and Trails)

John and I ate dinner at the old Virginian Hotel in Medicine Bow and the food was good there. It was completed in 1911, but it was under construction at least a few years prior to that. We spent the night in what used to be the local bank (or store) back in the day. You can see it in the photo on the left behind the old hotel.

Restored Train Depot at Medicine Bow
(Jay Harman photo, July 2016)

After we checked into the Virginian, we had a couple hours to kill, so we headed to Rock River. We wanted to go there because our grandmother, Pearl Slothower Harman, was born north of Rock River in 1904. There wasn't a whole lot to see in Rock River, but it was still on my list because it was an important town to my great-grandfather back during the homestead days, and he mentioned it several times in his life story. However, I should add that there was still a nostalgic charm about the place.

(Jay Harman photo, July 2016)

Jay Harman in front of Rock River sign in 2016

John Harman and Rock River First National Bank (built in 1919) (Jay Harman photo, July 2016)

Rock River Pool Hall and Bath House (middle), 1921 photo (Wyoming Tales and Trails)

Rock River Pool Hall building today, 2016 JRH photo

Railroad Station at Rock River, Wyoming, 1901 (Stimson Collection, STIM/268, Wyoming State Archives)

Going to Garrett

It was quite an adventure getting to Garrett. The next morning, we drove several miles east toward Rock River but turned off onto a dirt/slightly graveled road a few miles before getting to Rock River. Then we headed north and drove about twenty-eight miles to get to Garrett. We passed a huge reservoir and saw some "wide open" country and a lot of antelope and some cattle along the way. After all, this is ranch country.

Antelope by Wheatland Reservoir
(Jay Harman photo, July 2016)

Cattle near Wheatland Reservoir
(Jay Harman photo, July 2016)

About eight miles before arriving at Garrett, we came to a vantage point with an awesome view that made me wonder if this was what Great-grandfather Robert saw the first time he came into this country in 1891 or 1892. I believe we were still on Palmer Canyon Road and facing north when I took this picture. In his book, Robert gives the impression that he came up from Cheyenne, and he said that he passed through the McGill ranch and what is now a huge reservoir. The McGill Ranch is now the Flying X Ranch, and the reservoir was probably the Wheatland Reservoir, the one we passed to our right as we drove in from the south. It's really something to think about how it must have been for a young man in his twenties, who had set out on his own on horseback, to come into remote rugged county like this to find a new home and make a living.

By the way, this part of Wyoming is still very rugged and remote, somewhat like it was a hundred years ago, except now the ranchers have electricity and four-wheel drive pickups. Internet and cell phone reception is sketchy; it's still a different world even now!

About ten miles southeast of Garrett
(Jay Harman photo, July 2016)

When we rolled into Garrett, all there was to see was a bridge going over a small river, an older single-wide mobile home and a one-room schoolhouse, but soon some of the Garretts showed up. The Garretts were in the middle of haying up on Cow Creek near Great-grandfather Robert's homestead. Roger and Tom Garrett were in the process of moving some items out of Tom's old place because he had just sold it to Tom Dunlap. Anyone who has read Robert's story knows that the Garretts were valued neighbors to the young Slothowers, and Robert talks about their grandparents (T. S. and Mary A. Garrett) with great respect and appreciation in the book.

*North Laramie River from the bridge at Garrett
(Jay Harman photo, July 2016)*

One-room schoolhouse at Garrett
(Jay Harman photo, July 2016)

After greeting the Garretts, the next thing we got to see was the old post office and a log structure that the Slothowers had built up the road on the Cow Creek homestead, but it had been moved to the Garrett's ranch headquarters many years ago. Great-grandfather Robert was periodically in charge of the mail circuit around Garrett, but many of the local ranchers took their turn with this duty back in the day.

Tom Garrett (one of T. S. Garrett's grandsons) is standing in front of the old post office building which is now part of the Roger Garrett place, and I'm guessing it's been there since the beginning. I'm not sure, but I think Tom said it was built around 1903.

Tom Garrett in front of old Garrett Post Office
(Jay Harman photo, July 2016)
Permission by Thomas Garrett of Wheatland, Wyoming

I believe Tom told me that his father took him and his brother Roger to visit Elmer (Robert's younger brother) in Orchards in Washington State back when they were kids. I think this may have been back in the 1940s.

Old Garrett Post Office (Jay Harman photo, July 2016)

Mary Garrett and T. S. Garrett. TS in field on the ranch in the 1920s

Robert talked about Mary and T. S. Garrett in his "life story." They were wonderful neighbors, and they jumped right in to help out when one of the neighbors needed a hand. Whether it be when someone got sick or someone was having a baby or someone got stranded in a winter blizzard, or giving advice on the best spot to build a homestead cabin, they were always willing to help! Mary was a "trailblazer" for women back in the day. She had been raised in England before coming to the United States, and she was well-educated. She was the postmaster for Rock Creek in 1888 and then a few years later in Garrett and the justice of the peace in 1902, which was ground breaking for women at the time! Mary was also an excellent marksman and even had her own brand. She was the midwife who assisted with the delivery of two of Robert's children. One of them was my Uncle Fred, and I reconnected with two of his sons here in Oregon in 2017.

Mary Garrett helped to deliver two of my great-uncles. Left to right, Fred Slothower and Robert Jr. Gray Slothower.

I should mention another curious connection with the Garrett family. And this one is related to Mary and T. S. Garrett's youngest child, Mary Garrett Swan. The little girl in the photo below is little Mary (age about eight) along with her teacher, Emma Brandle Lamb. The photo was taken in 1910. Mary was only two years older than my grandmother Pearl Slothower, and they lived just a few miles apart. I'm sure they knew one another, and after discovering this photo, I began to wonder if they went to school together on the Garrett Ranch. Incidentally, the log cabin in the photo was the Garrett family's first residence on the homestead and was built around 1890.

Above photo courtesy of Julia Butler, Cow-Belles Ring School Bells, 1976

Tom Garrett had told me about the log structure (next page) that had been moved from the Slothower homestead, so I was excited to see it. Whether the cabin was built by Aaron or Robert is still a little unclear. Tom had told me that the dovetail joints on the structure were remarkable and somewhat unique to the area. Great-grandfather Robert built several log cabins back in the homestead days; he even built log cabins for each of Felix Atkinson's three brothers. It made all the more sense when I told Tom that as a young man and while still living in Denver with his parents, Robert did millwork and worked as an apprentice cabinetmaker. This log structure is at least 108 years old.

*Log cabin built by the Slothowers back
in the homestead days. (Roof not original)
(Jay Harman photo, July 2016)*

*Impressive dovetail joints (following page)
all done by hand with a saw and a broadax*

PLAINS TO THE PACIFIC

(Photo courtesy of Celia Otte Corson)

The above photo is the old-time barn on the Bell-Otte Ranch located northwest of Garrett. According to one of the locals, the barn was built by the Slothowers. My brother and I didn't see the barn on this trip. However, a few months after the Wyoming trip, the above photo was shared with me on Facebook by Celia Otte Corson. In her post, she commented, "My grandmother had always said their old red barn had been built by a man named Slothower." In all likelihood, the barn was built sometime between 1902 and 1910, so it's at least 108 years old. Just another example to support my theory that the Slothowers were accomplished builders back in the day.

Robert's Homestead

A little while later, my brother and I left Roger Garrett's place and headed up the dirt road to Robert's homestead on Cow Creek, now Tom Dunlap's place. The ranch is just over seven thousand feet in elevation, and the winters are harsh here. The last few miles of road going into the homestead is pretty rough, as in four-wheel-drive rough, and sometimes a snowmobile is the mode during the winter.

The rough dirt road also goes through some private property, so I'm glad I had permission ahead of time. Tom Dunlap is a descendant of another local pioneer family; as a matter a fact, he grew up on what was once Robert's homestead. I'm very grateful to Tom Dunlap and brothers Tom and Roger Garrett for inviting me to come to the ranch to look around for remnants and features of Robert's homestead. There are still some things that I'd like to investigate, so I hope I can go back there sometime in the future.

Bridge over Cow Creek in front of Robert's homestead cabin site (Jay Harman photo, July 2016)

In the above photo, you can see the bridge over Cow Creek Robert talks about in his life story when he recalls the last time he saw his mother before she moved to Oregon and passed away in 1911. Robert reflects on this part of his life at the end of the Wyoming chapter of his story as he looks at it one final time before leaving Wyoming for good in June of 1910.

Lower photo shows Tom Dunlap and Roger Garrett, both descendants of pioneer ranch families from the Garrett area. Both excellent people and full of the local history.

Tom Dunlap (left) and Roger Garrett (right)

Roger's grandfather, T. S. Garrett, was a local rancher and neighbor friend to all three of the Slothower brothers back during the homestead years.

Tom Dunlap standing next to "Slothower baby graves"
(Jay Harman photo, July 2016; permission by Tom Dunlap)

We were able to locate the Slothower baby graves with the help of Tom Dunlap. He remembered his dad talking about the graves from way back when he was a kid. He also matched things up from the description in the book, and you can still see a couple of very old wooden posts. I had a headstone made and took it with me on my second trip to the Wyoming homesteads in June 2018.

*Vintage building on Robert Slothower homestead
(Jay Harman photo, July 2016; permission by Tom Dunlap)*

This old building was on the place. Tom Dunlap told me that it was not originally there but had been moved from another location around Garrett (I think). I liked the look of it, so I snapped a picture. I'm guessing that it was built back in the 1920s. It would be interesting to know where it came from. It seems that they did a lot of moving of buildings back in the day.

Dollie and Robert Rock (Jay Harman photo, July 2016)

This is the rock from which Robert and Dollie sat together and viewed the progress on the homestead. Yes, right out of the book.

PLAINS TO THE PACIFIC

ROBERT SLOTHOWER HOMESTEAD

1906

2016

Robert's homestead in more recent times.
(Jay Harman photo, July 2016)

The previous photo shows what they would see today if looking toward the old homestead from their rock vantage point. None of the original buildings still stand, but the rest would probably look very familiar to them. Tom told me that the log home that Robert had built on the homestead back around 1901 had burned down many years ago. Tom went on to say that his mother was at home at the time the fire broke out and jumped on her horse in a panic with hair and clothes flying to go get help. So the house built by Robert is gone, but Tom showed me the remains of the stone foundation where it once stood.

The "Grandpa Place." Another Garrett area homestead (Jay Harman photo, July 2016)

This is what the Dunlaps call "The Grandpa Place" because this is where their grandfather (Harry Dunlap) lived back in the early 1900s. Remote and hidden away, it's a beautiful little mountain valley with its green hayfields and the Laramie Mountains for a backdrop. If you study the photo carefully, you can see the picturesque craftsman-style home built around 1900. It is truly a special sight! This picture was taken facing north and just a short distance from the "Robert and Dollie" rock.

Out of the old homesteads with buildings still standing, this one is the farthest up Cow Creek and is just north of Robert's old homestead. I was told that the old ranch house is now abandoned, but if you go inside, it doesn't quite feel that way, as there are still dishes in the old kitchen cabinets. They were cutting hay in the field to the left of the old house at the time I took the picture.

The original homesteader on the "Grandpa Place" was an Englishman by the name of Carleton Skarratt who lived here at the time Robert was here. Skarratt and my great-grandfather were acquaintances with another English homesteader by the name of Arthur G. B. Ternan, and there is a story about this young man being struck and killed by lightning that I will share with you in a section to follow.

Elmer Slothower's Homestead

This is how Elmer's old homestead looks today. The photo below gives you an idea as to how it looks as you drive in from the west and shortly after you begin to drop down. You can see the top of Laramie Peak in the background (just over ten thousand feet in elevation). The ranch headquarters is down in a small river valley, and the North Laramie River flows through this part of the ranch. As you can see, it is both beautiful and rugged.

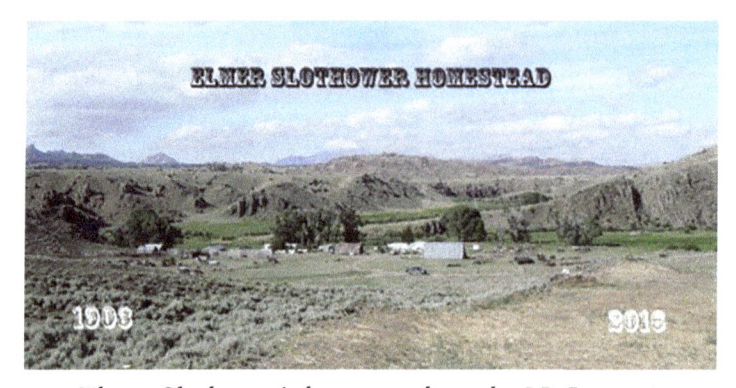

Elmer Slothower's homestead on the N. Laramie River near Garrett (Jay Harman photo, July 2016)

It is now the William Sturgeon Ranch. I really appreciated William and his son James for taking time to visit with me and show me around; they seemed to be rather interested in ranch history, just like me. If I would have come in five minutes later, I would have missed them as they were just driving out, so I got lucky, and it topped off the day's trip nicely!

Jay Harman with William Sturgeon (John Harman photo, July 2016)

It was great to have a chance to visit with William; his grandmother knew the Slothowers back in the day, and William shared a couple old Slothower stories with me. He also told me that Elmer's name is still on some of the water rights documents, and that some remnants of Elmer's rather amazing engineering as related to the old time irrigation system were still visible around the ranch. William also told me that T. S. Garret, who was Elmer's neighbor at the time, advised Elmer to not build his house down on a lower spot closer to the river. Elmer took his advice and this was around 1901.

Log structure built by Elmer Slothower
(Jay Harman photo, July 2016)

This is the only building still standing from the days when Elmer homesteaded here, well over a hundred years old. As you can see, the roof is not original. William told me the old Slothower home burned to the ground several years ago.

Elmer's registered cattle brand burned into window board

William had his son, James, go inside the old log building to retrieve something. It was an old window board that Elmer had built back in the day (above photo). Someone had burned Elmer's brand into it many years ago. The brand was registered around 1901.

This was a special adventure for my brother John and I, and I'm glad we did it! However, if I ever go back there, I will probably fly to Laramie and then rent a four-wheel-drive rig. Thanks again to Tom Dunlap, Roger and Tom Garrett, William and James Sturgeon, for taking time to visit with us and show us around the two old homesteads.

Second Trip to the Wyoming Homesteads
June 2018

Debra Harman photo taken about three miles south of Rock River, Wyoming, June 2018

In June 2018, I made my second trip to Albany County, Wyoming; the sacred land where six of my ancestors homesteaded, including my great-grandfather Robert. My wife (Deb) accompanied me on this one. There was a little more to this trip than the one in 2016 because I was going to be the keynote speaker for a presentation at the Rock River School. The theme for the presentation was "Early Homesteaders of North Albany County." I was grateful that the ladies from the Albany County Historic Society were able to make the arrangements, and we had a very nice turnout.

Two of the local ranchers who were also descendants of early homesteaders took part in the presentation as well. They were Dale Robbins and Jim Atkinson, and their grandparents knew my great-grandfather back around 1900 during the homesteading years.

Tom and Ronel Dunlap's place on Cow Creek near Garrett, Wyoming. Once Robert Slothower's homestead. Photo by Debra Harman, June 2018

To top it all off, Deb and I received three invitations to visit some of the historic homestead ranches that had a connection to Robert's life story and the Wyoming chapter. Unfortunately, we were only able to accept two of the invites due to time constraints. After all, we had a wedding to attend up near Missoula in a few days.

As I've said before, I love these kind of adventures! It's like going back in time, and when I see this part of

Wyoming and meet the people back there, it brings Robert's story even more to life. It's awesome!

In the following photo, I'm with my two Garrett friends, Tom and Ronel Dunlap. We're at the grave site where Great-grandfather Robert's first two babies are buried. As you can see, their two dogs posed perfectly for the picture! I had made a promise to create some kind of headstone for the gravesite the last time I was there. Great-grandfather had probably put some kind marker on the graves back at the time of burial, but it had long since turned to dust. After we got things situated, I said a little prayer over the graves.

(Tom and Ronel Dunlap, left, with author Jay Harman at the Slothower baby grave site on the Robert Slothower homestead. Photo by Debra Harman, June 2018)

*Dale Robbins, left, with author, Jay Harman in
June 2018; photo by Debra Harman.*

Here I am with Dale Robbins, fellow descendant of North Albany County Wyoming homesteaders. We stopped off on our way to the Cameron homestead. In the photo, Dale is pointing out the old townsite of Marshall.

*Elizabeth Marshall on left. Source: Ancestry.com.
Public domain, Ann (Cole) Kreister photo, circa 1905.
Marshall house on right courtesy of Dale Robbins.*

In the previous photo, Mrs. Elizabeth Marshall is focused on her needlepoint in her Marshall home in about 1905. Mrs. Marshall attended my great-grandparents wedding at the William Cameron homestead near Marshall in February of 1902.

Remains of William Cameron log cabin near Marshall, Wyoming. Dale Robbins on left, Jay Harman on right. My great-grandparents Robert and Dollie were married here in 1902. Photo by Debra Harman, June 2018.

Originally the William Cameron log cabin (my second great-grandfather). Later, Shuckey Bell's OO7 Ranch House. Ed and Anna Curry in front. Now part of the Dale Robbins Ranch. Photo courtesy of Dale Robbins.

Dale and Saundra Robbins at their home near Marshall, Wyoming. We had a wonderful visit with them. Beautiful ranch but definitely "off the grid." Photo by Debra Harman, June 2018.

Jim Atkinson speaking at the Rock River, Wyoming, presentation in June 2018. Shown on the screen on the left side is a picture of his grandparents, Lizzy and Felix Atkinson.

Lizzy and Felix Atkinson were important figures during Robert's early days in Wyoming, and he worked for them on their "Red Desert Ranch" for two years right around 1900. Robert helped to construct their irrigation system and built three log-cabin-style homes for Felix and his brothers.

Jim Atkinson, left, and Jay Harman at the Rock River, Wyoming, presentation in June 2018. Photographed by Debra Harman.

Log cabin built by Robert Slothower around 1900. It was originally built as a home for one of Felix Atkinson's brothers. Today the cabin sits on the Jim Atkinson Ranch near Marshall, Wyoming. Photo courtesy of Ronel Dunlap.

Jay and Deb Harman happy to be in Casper for dinner after a long drive from the Robbins Ranch. June 2018.

After leaving the Robbins Ranch near Marshall, Wyoming, we drove on unimproved dirt roads for several hours before we found pavement. Dale had given us a map he'd sketched and we pulled an old GPS out of the glovebox, but still at times, we weren't even sure if we were on the right road.

From Tea and Crumpets to Sage and Lightning

I found a very curious connection between several of the North Albany County homesteaders, who they were, and where they immigrated from. They were my great-grandfather's neighbors and part of his story during his Wyoming years. It was not surprising to discover that a high percentage of them had sailed across the Atlantic from England to make America their new home; most of us already know that.

Some of them came to North Albany County, Wyoming, to Rock Creek as early as the mid-1880s. What was surprising to me was that they chose this remote part of Wyoming, and many were not your ordinary Englishmen or Englishwomen! Perhaps it's not too dissimilar from when the British first settled in parts of Africa, Australia, New Zealand, and other remote and environmentally challenging parts of the world.

Some of these British immigrants were graduates of prestigious universities like Cambridge, some came from remarkable British military families, and one became the first woman to serve as justice of the peace in this part of Wyoming. My great-grandfather Robert knew most of them from the Garrett and Marshall communities. You may recall that he was there from 1892 to 1910. Although he did go back to Denver for a year in 1893.

In this next section, I'm going to focus on just three of them: Arthur G. B. Ternan, Carleton Skarrett, and Mary Banner Garrett. I should also mention that the man (Felix Atkinson) whom my great-grandfather Robert worked for back around 1900 was another English immigrant. This was when Robert was working on the "Red Desert Ranch," and this is where Robert met his wife-to-be, Dollie Cameron, my great-grandmother.

Felix Atkinson and Mary Banner Garrett immigrated to America from England in 1884. Skarratt immigrated in 1891, and Ternan immigrated around 1901.

Killed by Lightning Story

(theoretical image of Ternan on left)

While homesteading in Wyoming, my great-grandfather Robert was acquainted with a young Englishman and fellow homesteader by the name of Arthur G. B. Ternan. Robert called Arthur Ternan a "remittance man" in his memoir because he was being supported by his father back in England. Robert gave the impression that the man wasn't much of a worker and was just waiting for a rich uncle from down in Australia to "kick the bucket." Then one day, Ternan received a post informing him that his rich uncle had finally died, so the young Englishman (Ternan) was thrilled about his upcoming inheritance. Not too long after that, Ternan was killed by lightning while on a return trip from Laramie. They didn't find his body for almost a week. As you will see, the way he died is rather bizarre! Ternan had been visiting a doctor-friend of his and a school teacher he'd been courting in Laramie. Note: Above image of young man, not actually of Arthur Ternan.

Here's that story: A few months later after reading this passage in Robert's life story, I became more curious about this young Englishman. I discovered many remarkable things about Ternan. First of all, he was from a very prestigious British military family. His father, grandfather, some uncles, and at least one brother were all officers in the British Army. His grandfather had been a brigadier general. Arthur's father, Colonel Trevor Patrick Breffney Ternan (1917 photo to right) was a highly decorated officer and a hero of many campaigns that spanned from Afghanistan to Africa. Some of his medals were presented to him by King George in 1917. Related to this is that Arthur Ternan was actually born in India, not England. This was no doubt during a time when his father was serving there in the British Army, perhaps when he was military governor of one of the Indian provinces.

There is some confusion as to the location of Ternan's homestead. My great-grandfather's recollection in the book is that Ternan had his homestead right above his on Cow Creek. However, the "Death by Lightning" story in the July 4 edition of the 1907 *Laramie Republican* makes it sound like Ternan's homestead was just below the south side of Laramie Peak and not far from Fish Creek. This information would make the location something like fifteen miles (or more) northeast of Robert's homestead, but still in the Garrett neighborhood. To further complicate my research, I began to realize that some of these early settlers had more than one homestead. However, there was another Englishman homesteading directly above Robert's homestead on Cow Creek, and that was Carleton Skarratt.

Skarratt homestead house. Photo source, Albany County, Wyoming Assessor's website, 2013

The house pictured above was built by Skarratt back around 1900. If you look closely at the photo, you can tell that the place, back in "the day," must have been an exquisite example of the "craftsman style." The remoteness of this place adds to its charm. One of the local descendants (Tom Dunlap) told me in 2018 that there are logs underneath the exterior, so this may not have been exactly how it looked in 1902. Still love it though, …it's that going-back-in-time thing again!

I was also told by one of the locals (Ronel Dunlap) in June 2018 that Skarratt never had to pay for the building materials because there was no longer a record of the transaction. Evidently, the mercantile where he had purchased the materials (probably in Laramie) had burnt down after they had already delivered the materials.

Since Skarratt is part of the Arthur Ternan story, I'll give you a little more background on him and the Garrett community. Skarratt immigrated from England in about 1891 and was a teamster in Rock Creek in the late 1890s before spending more time on his homestead to raise cattle. Skarratt was also an officer in the local cattleman's association. Skarratt received his homestead patent for the land right above Great-grandfather Robert's in 1902. There was a lot going on around Garrett this particular year. 1902 was the same year T. S. Garrett (another friend of Robert's) received his patent for his place just a few miles away on the North Laramie River. In addition, this is the same year Robert brought his young bride home to his homestead on Cow Creek, just below Mr. Skarratt's place. In other words, all these early settlers (Englishman included) had to have known one another.

Ternan was a friend or at least an acquaintance of Skarratt's. As it turns out, these two Englishmen had some interesting things in common besides both having immigrated from England. For one, Skarratt was also an "upper class" Brit, being a man of resources and having graduated from Cambridge in England. Cambridge (then and now) is one of the most prestigious universities in Europe. In 1903, when there was a financial disagreement between young Ternan and his father, it was Skarratt who served as the "go between" to smooth things out. To me, this implies that there was a good chance Skarratt knew Arthur Ternan's father from earlier days in England.

I also found some rather interesting "twists and turns" especially as related to the timing of when Arthur Ternan supposedly wrote his will. Case in point, it was Carleton Skarratt who showed up with Ternan's will claiming that Arthur Ternan had written it (with Skarratt's legal guidance) *just three weeks* before his death. At a minimum, very curious timing. In addition, Ternan had a $3,000 life insurance policy which would be considered unusual for the times, especially in Wyoming. Ternan had also become a third-degree Mason in Laramie just a few weeks before his death.

Ternan's body was found alongside the road about twenty-eight miles north of Laramie near the end of the Bosler line. Interesting to note that the two horses hitched to Arthur Ternan's buggy completely survived the lightning strike unharmed and still had their harnesses on when a young ranch hand found them near the Diamond Ranch.

The coroner's inspection of the body mentioned in the 1907 *Laramie Republican* newspaper article sounds convincing. Evidentially, *the bolt of lightning struck his head and went right down through the core of his body and through the seat of his buggy to ground.* Kind of incredible to think of the odds of being struck by lightning like that. The lightning bolt even melted some gold coins in his pocket and the gold fob on his fancy pocket watch which captured the time of his death at 5:17! Young Ternan was only twenty-seven years old when he died, and he was buried in Laramie. Ternan immigrated to the United States in about 1901, so he was only twenty-one when he first came to America (probably by himself).

I should mention that I have now heard of or read about other people and livestock being killed or severely injured by lightning in this part of the country. As mentioned in Robert's memoir, my great-grandmother Dollie Cameron Slothower was deathly afraid of lightning, and her older sister was killed by lightning. Ronel Dunlap (a friend of mine from Garrett) told me that one of her Bennett relatives met the same fate up around Marshall several years ago. This Marshall area cowboy had a premonition that he would die with his reins in his hands, and that's just how they found him along with his dead horse. Dale Robbins (a friend of mine from Marshall) was there when the coroner arrived to inspect the body. Lightning makes a mess of the human body, but if you receive a direct hit by a lightning bolt, it's probably a quick way to "meet your maker."

Mary A. Banner Garrett

Robert talks about his high regard for the Garretts at the end of the "Wyoming" chapter. You may recall that while Robert was homesteading in Wyoming, Mary Garrett helped to deliver two of Robert's children. I added further details on the Garretts in the "First Trip to the Homesteads" section in the book. My great-grandfather and his two brothers were fellow homesteaders and friends of the Garrett family.

Mary Garrett was ahead of her time with her accomplishments in Wyoming. As mentioned earlier, she was one of the first women to be elected justice of peace in the United States. She also served as postmaster in Garrett. She was well-educated and not afraid to take on new challenges beyond her priority, which was raising her six children. Mary Garrett even received two land patents, one in 1908 and one in 1925. Mary was such an exceptional individual, that there was a write-up about her in the *Chicago American* in 1903.

In the election mentioned above (in late 1902), my great-uncle Elmer Slothower (a neighboring rancher) was elected to serve as constable to work with Justice Garrett. The following article will give you an idea as to what justice was like in the Wyoming hills under Justice Garrett.

(Following article: Mary A. Garrett court case transcribed from the Laramie Boomerang, *Feb. 10, 1904)*

ROBERT J. SLOTHOWER AND JAMES R. HARMAN

Law on the North Laramie
An Interesting Legal Controversy Going on There
Matter of a Peace Proceeding

Justice has to Decide if a Man Can Swear Himself in as an Attorney—Arguments are Lengthy.

Northern Albany is a very progressive part of the county in many ways, and in no way more so than in the manner in which it conducts its legal controversies.

A case in point is the legal proceedings which recently grew out of alleged threats made by Olsie Centers the son of William Centers of Cow Creek, against the peace and welfare of the young son of Mrs. Garrett of Garrett.

Mrs. Garrett is a justice of the peace herself, and it was a much-mooted question for some days among the ranchmen around Garrett, whether she could swear out a peace warrant before herself. After much consultation and earnest research through various pretentious volumes which occupy a conspicuous place in Mrs. Garrett's office, it was decided by a counsel assembled for the purpose that she could not, and accordingly she drove over to the ranch of the neighboring justice, Mr.

Edholm of Toltec, and there swore out a peace warrant against Olsie Centers.

The serving of the peace warrant was a serious business but was finally undertaken by Westley Hall. It is said that Mr. Hall, not being very well up in legal proceedings, handed the warrant to the father of Olsie Centers, who promptly stuck it in the stove and the discomfited special officer had to ride back to Garrett for advice. A second warrant was made out and Mr. Hall again essayed to serve it. Having been coached as to his duty Mr. Hall proceeded to read the warrant to Mr. Centers and his son.

Half way through the reading something happened, it is not clear what, but Mr. Hall rode home with a bad cut upon the side of his head, caused it by a fall when he was running, says one report, while another report says that a monkey-wrench with a man at the end of it had something to do with the accident.

On the day set for the return of the warrant there was a goodly crowd at the office of the Justice of the Peace for the Toltec precinct, news of the case having got abroad. Mr. Centers and his son arrived on time and so did Mrs. Garrett. The justice was a little late, but assumed his judicial bench within half an hour set for the trial to begin.

Proceedings were interesting from the first when Mr. Carleton Skarrett of the Skarrett ranch on Cow Creek informed the justice that he appeared as attorney for Mr. Olsie Centers. Mrs. Garrett immediately objected. Arguments we heard upon both sides some of the speeches being quite lengthy and the evening shadows were lengthening when the justice decided that Mr. Skarrett, not being admitted to the bar of Albany county, could not act as an attorney for anybody.

Mr. Skarrett, who is a man of many resources, thereupon offered to swear himself in as an attorney. This action upon the part of Mr. Skarrett was a facer for the court, but after hearing more lengthy arguments from both Mrs. Garrett and Mr. Skarrett, he decided to adjourn court until he had thought it over.

Upon the resumption of the court next morning Mr. Centers moved that the case be again adjourned while the Justice thought the matter over a little more and obtained some advice. After a few arguments upon this latest motion the case was continued until the afternoon. In the afternoon when the court was called to order, Mrs. Garrett made a motion that the case be tried by a jury. This motion caused much more argument and much more consulting of legal volumes sent from Mrs. Garrett's house and lent by neighbors.

It was finally agreed that a list of a dozen residents of the Toltec precinct be prepared by the justice, with the help of Mrs. Garrett and Mr. Skarrett and that the list be forwarded to the County Prosecuting Attorney, with the request that he select three persons from the list to try the case. The list and the request was duly received by the prosecuting attorney, who informed Judge Edholm that a jury could not be asked for in a peace proceeding.

There the matter rests at present and the North Laramie country is waiting anxiously for the next move on the part of the various legal luminaries of the district.

Robert's Family and the Civil War

The contribution made by many of Robert's relatives during the Civil War was significant! I believe that their service and sacrifice had an influence on Robert's character. As I've dug deeper with my research, it's been both enlightening and remarkable to begin to realize that Robert's family members were right in the middle of this incredible life and nation-changing struggle. *The background photo shown above is of the John D. Slothower Pre-Civil War Farm in Southern Pennsylvania. Courtesy of Jeffrey and Tina Gleim of Wellsville, PA.*

John D. Slothower (Robert's grandfather) did not lose any sons in the Civil War, but he did lose three horses. Some of General Jeb Stuart's cavalry soldiers came through the Slothower farm in early July of 1863 and confiscated three of their horses. Hard to imagine what it must have been like for John D. and Mary on the day the Confederate soldiers showed up on their horses, armed with sabers and sidearms, and demanded they relinquish their horses. Must have been very stressful, considering that John D. had a wife and several children to protect. However, this episode pales in comparison to what happened to Robert's other grandfather.

When I think about how little of this information was known or passed down to generations to follow, it's a little hard to believe. Sometimes I feel like my ancestors are reaching out to me in some unexplainable way to bring their story back to life to be shared and understood by the younger generations.

I was amazed to discover that in addition to Robert's father (Lewis), he had three uncles (Joseph, Jacob, and Henry), a father-in-law (William Cameron), and a grandfather (Joshua Chapman), who served in the Union Army during the war. They were all privates, except for Henry who mustered out as a corporal, and they were all from York County, Pennsylvania, except for William Cameron who was from Iowa. I've included details in the pages that follow on just three of them.

William R. Cameron, Iowa 8th Inf, Co. A, Robert's father-in-law

Another huge surprise was to learn that Robert's father's home county of York is adjacent to the county where one of the most important battles of the Civil War was fought, and that was *Gettysburg*, which began on Wednesday, July 1, 1863! As a matter of fact, Robert's grandfather, John D. Slothower, was baptized in Gettysburg. John D. had eight sons and one daughter, and *four* of his sons served in the Union army during the Civil War.

Further to that, it's important to note that there were two other battles or engagements in other nearby towns that took place a short distance from their home. These took place in Carlisle and Mechanicsburg. To give you a better idea as to how close their farm was to the war zone, they were only about eleven miles from Mechanicsburg and only about nineteen miles from Gettysburg.

Confederate forces shelled Carlisle and took it first and then moved on to Mechanicsburg and captured it with little or no resistance from Union forces. This took place shortly before the Battle of Gettysburg. Mechanicsburg is noted as the northernmost town that Confederate forces occupied. The other notable point is that Mechanicsburg is where Joshua Jackson Chapman (Robert's grandfather) enlisted in the spring of 1864. Joshua's story is the most tragic, as you will soon discover.

(Source: Civil War Trails website, http://www.pacivilwartrails.com)

Lewis B. Slothower *(Robert's father)*
Above photo, courtesy of Maxine Sullivan.
Above photo, Find a grave.com
Lewis served in "Company I" of the 209th Pennsylvania Volunteers

Lewis Slothower (Robert's father) enlisted when he was nineteen, and he served during the last year of the war beginning in 1864. Lewis's regiment was involved in the final campaign against Confederate forces protecting Richmond, Virginia. This march was on the Bermuda Hundred Peninsula in Virginia. This move by the Union Army was a prelude to the march on Richmond. After a failed attempt to move on the confederate forces protecting Richmond, both sides dug trenches, and it remained a stalemate for the remainder of the war. In Robert's story in the Denver chapter, he mentions that his father was a Civil War veteran and that he had slept next to graveyards while serving during the Civil War. Lewis is buried in the Riverside Soldiers Cemetery in Denver, Colorado. *(Source: Civil War Trust, www.civilwar.org/civil-war-discovery-trail)*

The following photo reflects Lewis's (Robert's father) and his Uncle Joseph's involvement in the "Great Rebellion." Both Lewis and Joseph served in "Company I" in the 209th Pennsylvania Volunteers in 1864 and the first part of 1865. Their names appear on the document below.

Photo of original commemorative document, published January 1865 by Fuller and Co., Baltimore, Maryland, courtesy of Barbara Higinbotham

An interesting detail on Joseph's service record is that he actually deserted his unit for a period of time during the last year of the war but then returned on his own without consequences; at least none were provided in the military records. I was unable to find the reason for his temporary desertion or why his commanding officer showed him so much leniency. He got lucky, and there must have been some very good reason.

Joshua Jackson Chapman *(Robert's grandfather)*
Died in Andersonville Prison in Georgia in 1864

Joshua Jackson Chapman and his Company's Story in the Civil War

The 7th Pennsylvania Reserves/36th Volunteers Company H was first recruited in Cumberland County, Pennsylvania, in May 1861; however, a smaller group including Joshua Chapman was recruited in February 1864. Military records say that he was five feet seven inches tall, had a light complexion, and had light hair. He was about forty-two years old at the time he enlisted in the army, so he was not a young man. Joshua's rank was private. He was under the command of Captain Samuel B. King.

Robert never knew his grandfather Joshua Chapman due to the fact that his father, Lewis, married Joshua's daughter Eliza, two years after Joshua died in the notorious Andersonville prisoner of war camp in Georgia. However, it is very likely that Robert had heard some of the family history from his mother.

Another incredible thing about Joshua Chapman's story has to do with the reason why he enlisted. Back during the Civil War, the government had a policy whereby a man who was drafted could get out of serving if he found a substitute and paid him $300. My research seems to indicate that Joshua enlisted as a substitute presumably because he had a large family, and they were "flat out" poor. So, in other words, he did it to get money for his family. Joshua had a wife and seven children at home.

If you look at his military service dates going from enlistment (February 13, 1864) to his death in Andersonville Prison on July 1, 1864, he didn't really last that long. After his capture, he lasted less than two months.

Joshua was captured and taken prisoner on May 5, 1864 during a large scale three-day battle known as the Battle of the Wilderness in Spotsylvania County, Virginia. This was the first major campaign directed by Ulysses S. Grant after President Lincoln gave him command of the entire Union Army.

Grant went against Robert E. Lee's forces. The fighting was fierce and made even more difficult because of the smoke, trees, and the dense underbrush. The outcome of the battle was inconclusive, but Grant did force Lee to retreat. There were heavy losses on both sides.

Battle of the Wilderness, May 6, 1864 (by Kurz and Allison, Library of Congress, Civil War Collection, cph.3g01748)

Joshua's company was "severely ravaged" during this battle but had also taken significant losses in earlier battles, including Antietam and Fredericksburg. This was *not* a "light duty" unit that was kept in the rear away from combat during the Civil War.

There were 8 officers and 117 enlisted men in Company H. Here are the company's statistics.

11—Killed in action, one by "friendly fire"

5—Died from disease or from their wounds

21—Release on medical discharge due to wounds or disease

6—Deserted or dishonorable discharge

23—Missing in action, mostly in the Battle of the Wilderness

25—Captured and taken prisoner, most of these during the Battle of the Wilderness. Of these, *nine died in*

Andersonville Prison, including Robert's grandfather, Joshua Jackson Chapman. He died of acute dysentery on July 1, 1864.

Out of 125 men and officers in this company, only 34 came out "unscathed," 91 didn't. A couple of their officers resigned and a couple enlisted men were transferred, so the data may be off slightly.

Andersonville Prison in Georgia was the most notorious prison in the South during the Civil War. It had a *28 percent mortality* rate. Out of approximately forty-five thousand men who came through its gates, almost thirteen thousand of them died there. The dead were buried in mass graves. The conditions there were horrendous. *(Sources for above: Find a Grave.com and Regimental History of the 7th Pennsylvania Reserves/36th Volunteers, Company H)*

Union Prisoners at ration wagon, Andersonville Prisoner of War Camp in Georgia, August 16, 1864 (Riddle photo #8, US Library of Congress, 4181–16)

The above photo was taken about a month after Robert's grandfather, Joshua Chapman, died at the camp. In reviewing military records, I found two different dates for his death at the camp: one was June 30, 1864, and the other one was July 1, 1864.

As you can see in the sketch below, there was a stream (more like an open ditch) that went down through the middle of the camp. This ditch served as the prisoners' drinking, bathing, and sewer water.

Andersonville Prisoner of War Camp,
Georgia during the Civil War, 1864
Original sketch by John L. Ransom, PGA—A. Sachse & Co.
United States Library of Congress

Jacob B. Slothower *(One of Robert's uncles)*

At twenty-six years of age, Jacob B. Slothower enlisted as a soldier to fight in the War of Rebellion. As far as I can determine, he must have been the *most "battle hardened"* of all Robert's Slothower relatives. My research seems to indicate that he may have participated in as many as sixteen heavy battles!

Jacob enlisted as a private on September 19, 1861. He mustered in Company H in the 87th Pennsylvania Volunteers on the same day of his enlistment. His army record extended over three years, and during that time, he participated in several major battles, among which were the Battle of the Wilderness, Spottsylvania, Cold Harbor, Petersburg, Winchester, and Fisher's Hill. Jacob mustered out on October 13, 1864.

Photo labels (top of photo):
- Robert's Great-grandson & author — Jay Harman
- Aaron's grandson — David Slothower
- Robert's grandson — Loran Slothower
- Elmer's grandson — Jim Slothower

Slothower descendants with birthday boys on right end (identified top of photo). The legacy lives on. Taken at Slothower family reunion summer 2017

Sources and Credits

Dennis Slothower (top left), David Slothower (top right), and Janice Dugan (bottom left) and Marie Nelson. Thanks to these Slothower cousins, Robert's story was passed on to me, making it possible for me to share it with you.

Deb Harman, my wife and chief editor

Photographs, Images, and Art

Civil War Collection Photos. Library of Congress, United States. Public domain photographs. www.loc.gov/pictures/collection/civwar/. Accessed 2016.

Cow-Belles Ring School Bells1976, Albany County Cow Belles Club, 1976

Denver Public Library, Western Collection, March 1894 photos of Denver City Hall Wars

Dugan, Janice. Family member who provided photographs. McMinnville, Oregon. 2015.

Fort D. A. Russell photo, University of Wyoming State Archives (Wikipedia) Nat. Park Serv and Nat Reg. of Historic Places

Franzen, Zach. *Boy on Horse* (watercolor). Permission granted via e-mail.

Graphics Factory. Paid subscription, royalty-free.

Harman, James Robert (Jay). Artwork and photographs of family and of Wyoming research trip. June 2016 and 2018.

Higinbotham, Barbara. Family member who provided photographs. Corvallis, Oregon. 2015.

Image of Slothower Homestead Information. Albany County Wyoming Historic Society, Laramie. Dicksie Knight May, researcher for the Albany County Historic Society, created the image. 2015.

Jenny, Slothower, Lael. Family member who provided photographs. 2015, 2016.

Land Records. Bureau of Land Management. glorerecords.blm.gov.search. Accessed 2015.

Maps. Wyoming Bureau of Land Management. Last update November 12, 2002. www.blm.gov/wy/st/en/resources/public_room.html. Accessed 2015.

Marvin Hall photo. Marvin 100 Year Anniversary Publication, Genealogy Room, Phillipsburg City Library, Kansas

McKnight, Bernard. Andersonville Prison (online biography of B. McKnight). Riddle photograph # 8: August 16, 1864.

http://www.wright.edu/~jack.mcknight/andersonville/cover.htm. Accessed 2015.

National Portrait Gallery of the United Kingdom.

Portrait of Col. Trevor Patrick Ternan, 1917, London, by Bassano Ltd, donation/permission

Peel, Maggie. Flake and Belle Hall photos, Cheyenne, Wyoming, June 2018.

Rock Creek ghost town photos and other. Wyoming Tales and Trails. www.wyomingtalesandtrails.com. 1999. Accessed December 22, 2015.

Settle Slothower, Bea. Family member who provided photographs. Oregon City, Oregon. 2015.

Sharp, Leslie, artist. West Linn, Oregon. Sketches commissioned for this book.

Shutterstock. Paid subscription, royalty free.

Slothower, Dennis. Family member who provided photographs and stories. 2015.

Sullivan, Maxine Slothower. Family member who provided photographs. 2015.

United States Bureau of Reclamation Archives, Grand Coulee Damn photo, 1942.

University of Wyoming American Heritage Center and State Archives. www.uwyo.edu/ahc/. Permission granted via e-mail in January 2017, John R. Waggener Associate Archivist. Accessed 2016.

Roy Partick homestead photos, Glenda Cates, Las Vegas, NV, 2019

Additional Sources and Credits

Ancestry.com. Census data. http://www.ancestry.com. Accessed 2015 and 2016.

Bates, Samuel P. (Samuel Penniman Bates). *1827-1902: History of Pennsylvania Volunteers, 1861-5; prepared in compliance with acts of the legislature.* http://www.pacivilwar.com/bates.html. Accessed 2015.

Boy falling through ice image, Royalty-Free (RF) End User License from ClipartOf.com, Aug. 2019

Civil War Discovery Trail. Civil War Trust. www.civilwar.org/civil-war-discovery-trail/. Accessed 2015.

Cameron, Barry—Civil War era photo of William R. Cameron

Civil War. *The Search for Battles.* National Park Service, The US Department of the Interior. www.nps.gov/civilwar/search-battles.htm. Accessed 2015.

Dage, Paul. Assisted with final phase editing. Deerhorn, OR.

Dyer, Frederick Henry. *A Compendium of the War of the Rebellion.* Dyer Publishing Company. Digitizing sponsor Emory University, manuscript. Des Moines, Iowa. 1908. Accessed 2015.

Find a Grave. *Joshua Jackson Chapman.* http://findagrave.com. Accessed 2015.

Gleim, Jeffrey and Tina of Wellsville, PA—John D. Slothower farm photo

Kansas Historical Society. *Grasshopper Plague of 1874.* June 2003, mod. October 2016. www.kshs.org/kansapedia/grasshopper-plague-of-1874/. Accessed 2015.

Knight, Dicksie May. Albany County Historic Society. Email correspondence, homestead information and newspaper articles

Kilmer, Joyce. *Trees.* August 1913, www.poetryfoundation.org. Accessed 2015

Loofbourow, Leslie. Preliminary editing, consulting. Milwaukie, Oregon.

Mikulec, Pat. Final phase editing and consulting. Colton, Oregon

Nebraska State Historic Society, photo by Solomon Butcher, Threshing with horses in Custer Co. Nebraska, 1887

Nelson, Marie. Several "old time" family photos, September, 2019, Brush Prairie, WA

Robbins, Dale and Saundra. Rock Creek photos, photos of Cameron homestead, Wyoming sunset photo, other historical information. Marshall, Wyoming

Sako, Lillian (Ancestry.com)—photo of William Taylor and related family history

Slothower, David G. Slothower genealogy research. Cape Coral, Florida. Resource assistance and telephone correspondence. Accessed 2015 and 2016.

Wyoming Newspapers, previously Wyoming Newspaper Project. Credit request on site: Wyoming Newspapers. Wyoming State Library. http://newspapers.wyo.gov/. Accessed 2015.

Wyoming State Archives Department of State Parks and Cultural Resources. Permission granted through permission forms and fee in January of 2017. wyarchives.state.wy.us. Accessed June 2015.

Yukon Archives. Finnie Family Fonds, 81/21 #465, Pho 141 Photo of men working on Canol Pipeline, Jan. 1944.

Of course, this project would not have come to light without the most important source of all, which is my great-grandfather's life story. Thank you, Great-grandfather Robert J. Slothower! Your story has inspired and motivated me beyond words.
James Robert Harman, December 16, 2018

*Some of Robert's descendants on the Harman side
(left to right are Mike, John, Philip, Joe, Jay, Jason)
(photo taken by DeWayne Williams 2013)*

About the Author

Author Jay Harman has been on a mission over the past six years. Drawn to discovering his roots, he has coauthored this book, traveled to England and Scotland to find an ancient church where his ancestors once worshiped and has visited a family homestead in remote Wyoming where his great-grandmother died during a winter blizzard in 1909.

Harman was born and raised in Corvallis, Oregon, and received his bachelor's degree from OSU in June 1979. He lives by a moral code built upon placing family first, relationships, and self-reliance; along with a tremendous respect for the great outdoors. The author is grateful to have chosen a career to serve young people and his community as a high school technology teacher for twenty-seven years.

Now retired from teaching, Harman and his wife, Debra, live on a small farm south of Canby, Oregon. Harman is just as happy to hop on his tractor to move his cattle to a new pasture as he is to research and write about family history. This is his first book.

Printed in the USA
CPSIA information can be obtained
at www.ICGtesting.com
JSHW011610281023
50969JS00007B/10/J

9 781685 268541